PENGUIN BOOKS

DEAD AID

Dambisa Moyo worked at Goldman Sachs for eight years, having previously worked for the World Bank as a consultant. Dambisa completed a PhD in Economics at Oxford University, and holds a Masters from Harvard University Kennedy School of Government. She was born and raised in Lusaka, Zambia.

D1059494

Dead Aid

Why Aid Makes Things Worse and How There is Another Way for Africa

DAMBISA MOYO

PENGUIN BOOKS

PENGUIN BOOKS

Published by the Penguin Group
Penguin Books Ltd, 80 Strand, London WC2R ORL, England
Penguin Group (USA) Inc., 375 Hudson Street, New York, New York 10014, USA
Penguin Group (Canada), 90 Eglinton Avenue East, Suite 700, Toronto, Ontario, Canada M4P 2Y3
(a division of Pearson Penguin Canada Inc.)
Penguin Ireland, 25 St Stephen's Green, Dublin 2, Ireland (a division of Penguin Books Ltd)
Penguin Group (Australia), 250 Camberwell Road, Camberwell, Victoria 3124, Australia
(a division of Pearson Australia Group Pty Ltd)
Penguin Books India Pvt Ltd, 11 Community Centre, Panchsheel Park, New Delhi – 110 017, India
Penguin Group (NZ), 67 Apollo Drive, Rosedale, North Shore 0632, New Zealand
(a division of Pearson New Zealand Ltd)
Penguin Books (South Africa) (Pty) Ltd, 24 Sturdee Avenue, Rosebank, Johannesburg 2196, South Africa

Penguin Books Ltd, Registered Offices: 80 Strand, London WC2R ORL, England

www.penguin.com

First published by Allen Lane 2009
Published in Penguin Books 2010
5

Copyright © Dambisa Moyo, 2009
Foreword © Niall Ferguson, 2009
All rights reserved

Typeset by Rowland Phototypesetting Ltd, Bury St Edmunds, Suffolk
Printed in England by Clays Ltd, St Ives plc

978-0-141-03118-7

www.greenpenguin.co.uk

Penguin Books is committed to a sustainable future
for our business, our readers and our planet.
The book in your hands is made from paper
certified by the Forest Stewardship Council.

Contents

To the Excellencies and officials of Europe: We suffer enormously in Africa. Help us. We have problems in Africa. We lack rights as children. We have war and illness, we lack food . . . We want to study, and we ask you to help us to study so we can be like you, in Africa.

Message found on the bodies of Guinean teenagers Yaguine Koita and Fode Tounkara, stowaways who died attempting to reach Europe in the landing gear of an airliner.

For Peter Bauer

Foreword
by Niall Ferguson

It has long seemed to me problematic, and even a little embarrassing, that so much of the public debate about Africa's economic problems should be conducted by non-African white men. From the economists (Paul Collier, William Easterly, Jeffrey Sachs) to the rock stars (Bono, Bob Geldof), the African discussion has been colonized as surely as the African continent was a century ago. The simple fact that *Dead Aid* is the work of an African black woman is the least of the reasons why you should read it. But it is a good reason nonetheless.

Born and educated in Zambia, Dambisa Moyo also brings to her subject a rare combination of academic expertise and 'real world' experience. Her training in economics took her from the World Bank to Harvard and on to Oxford, where she obtained her doctorate. Since leaving the academy, she has spent eight highly successful years at Goldman Sachs, most recently as Global Economist and Strategist. It is quite a CV.

And this is quite a book. Though she is not the first writer to criticize Western aid programmes in Africa, never has the case against aid been made with such rigour and conviction. Why, asks Moyo, do the majority of sub-Saharan countries 'flounder in a seemingly never-ending cycle of corruption, disease, poverty, and aid-dependency', despite the fact that their countries have received more than US$300 billion in development assistance since 1970, The answer she gives is that African countries are poor precisely *because* of all that aid. Despite the widespread Western belief that 'the rich should help the poor, and the form of this help should be aid', the reality is that aid has helped make the poor poorer, and growth slower. In Moyo's startling words: 'Aid has been, and continues to be, an unmitigated political, economic, and humanitarian disaster for most parts of the developing world.' In short, it is (as Karl Kraus said of Freudianism) 'the disease of which it pretends to be the cure'.

The correlation is certainly suggestive, even if the causation may be debated. Over the past thirty years, according to Moyo, the most aid-dependent countries have exhibited an average annual growth rate of *minus* 0.2 per cent. Between 1970 and 1998, when aid flows to Africa were at their peak, the poverty rate in Africa actually rose from 11 per cent to a staggering 66 per cent.

Why? Moyo's crucial insight is that the receipt of concessional (non-emergency) loans and grants has much same effect in Africa as the possession of a valuable natural resource: it's a kind of curse because it encourages corruption and conflict, while at the same time discouraging free enterprise.

Moyo recounts some of the more egregious examples of aid-fuelled corruption. In the course of his disastrous reign, Zaire's President Mobutu Sese Seko is estimated to have stolen a sum equivalent to the entire external debt of his country: US$5 billion. No sooner had he requested a reduction in interest payments on the debt than he leased Concorde to fly his daughter to her wedding in the Ivory Coast. According to one estimate, at least US$10 billion – nearly half of Africa's 2003 foreign aid receipts – leave the continent every year.

The provision of loans and grants on relatively easy terms encourages this kind of thing as surely as the existence of copious oil reserves or diamond mines. Not only is aid easy to steal, as it is usually provided directly to African governments, but it also makes control over government worth fighting for. And, perhaps most importantly, the influx of aid can undermine domestic saving and investment. She cites the example of the African mosquito net manufacturer who is put out of business by well-intentioned aid agencies doling out free nets.

Moyo offers four alternative sources of funding for African economies, none of which has the same deleterious side effects as aid. First, African governments should follow Asian emerging markets in accessing the international bond markets and taking advantage of the falling yields paid by sovereign borrowers over ᵁᵁᵁᵁᵁᵁ

the past decade. Second, they should encourage the Chinese policy of large-scale direct investment in infrastructure. (China invested US$900 million in Africa in 2004, compared with just US$20 million in 1975.) Third, they should continue to press for genuine free trade in agricultural products, which means that the US, the EU and Japan must scrap the various subsidies they pay to their farmers, enabling African countries to increase their earnings from primary product exports. Fourth, they should encourage financial intermediation. Specifically, they need to foster the spread of microfinance institutions of the sort that have flourished in Asia and Latin America. They should also follow the Peruvian economist Hernando de Soto's advice and grant the inhabitants of shanty towns secure legal title to their homes, so that these can be used as collateral. And they should make it cheaper for emigrants to send remittances back home.

In *Dead Aid*, Dambisa Moyo does not pull her punches. 'In a perfect world,' she writes, 'what poor countries at the lowest rungs of economic development need is not a multi-party democracy, but in fact a decisive benevolent dictator to push through the reforms required to get the economy moving.' In other words, rushing to elections before economic growth has got underway is a recipe for failure. But her most radical proposal comes in the form of a question. 'What if,' she asks, 'one by one, African countries each received a phone call . . . telling them that in exactly five years the aid taps would be shut off – permanently?'

The phrase 'shock therapy' fell into some disrepute in Eastern Europe in the 1990s. Yet that is precisely what Dambisa Moyo wants to give her African homeland. It may seem draconian. Yet it is worth remembering that, as she points out, 'just thirty years ago Malawi, Burundi and Burkina Faso were economically ahead of China on a per capita income basis'. Foreign direct investment and rapidly growing exports, not aid, have been the key to China's economic miracle. Africa needs to learn from Asia.

This is strong medicine that is being prescribed. But no one who reads *Dead Aid* will doubt that Dambisa Moyo's primary motivation is to reduce, not to increase, hardship. This is an African view of Africa's economic problems. The result is a book that manages to be, at one and the same time, hard-headed and big-hearted. This reader was left wanting a lot more Moyo, and a lot less Bono.

Preface

In July 1970, ninety students graduated from the University of Zambia, in the country's capital, Lusaka. Among them were the university's first black graduates (including some ten young women), and my parents were two of them. They were both studying for undergraduate degrees – my father reading linguistics, and my mother English. They came from different tribes, from different parts of rural colonial Africa: my father, the son of a miner in apartheid South Africa; my mother, the daughter of a man who would later train to be a teacher. My mother did not speak my father's language, and hence they mainly conversed in English. They met and married while still students.

Zambia (formerly known as Northern Rhodesia) had been independent from British colonial rule for just six years, and the excitement at the prospect of what amazing things lay ahead was palpable. Although, upon graduation, my mother had eleven job offers (at the time companies were very eager to employ black graduates), my father wished to continue his studies. He was offered a scholarship at the University of California at Los Angeles in the USA and, very soon afterwards, my parents packed up my sister and me and decamped to America. Our move was all planned. My parents' goal was for my father to further his education (later my mother would complete an advanced degree in Britain), and then return to Africa.

The 1970s were an exciting time to be African. Many of our nations had just achieved independence, and with that came a deep sense of dignity, self-respect and hope for the future. My parents lived, worked, and studied in the USA for eight years and upon my father's Ph.D. graduation, in 1978, they promptly moved back to Zambia, convinced that their future, and the futures of their children, lay in their homeland. My parents have never lived abroad again – remaining steadfastly committed to the view that they can help their country, their continent (contributing in their own small ways), to one day become politically and economically great. My mother has forged a career in banking – starting as the first Zambian woman bank manager, and rising to be Chairman of one of Zambia's leading banks. My father has stayed true to academia but has involved himself in broadcasting and also run an anti-corruption organization.

I spent my formative years in Zambia – primary, secondary, and tertiary school; ending up studying Chemistry at the same university as my parents seventeen years earlier. But in July 1990 my studies were interrupted by an attempted coup against the then President, Kenneth Kaunda. Although it didn't last long, the disruption was enough to shut the university down and have the students sent home. This would be the trigger for me to leave Zambia and, like my father before me, I ended up in the United States on a scholarship, eager to complete my higher education. And, like both my parents, I was certain that I would soon return.

I spent two years at the World Bank in Washington DC, two years doing a Master's at Harvard, and another four years completing a doctorate in Economics at Oxford. While away, I missed key moments in my country's history – our political move from one-party state to multi-party democracy in 1991 (it was the first former British colony in Africa to have its president removed by ballot rather than bullet), the overhaul of our economy from socialism to capitalism, and the tragic advent of the HIV–AIDS epidemic.

Although pulled by family and cultural ties in Zambia, every time I looked, prospects for my personal development appeared to diminish. There seemed to be fewer and fewer reasons for me to return, and more and more reasons for me to stay away. I could not help feeling that job opportunities commensurate with my education and experience lay not at home, but abroad. Those jobs that did exist at home (of course there were highly paid jobs available) were in an environment laden with creaking bureaucracy.

My best friend took a different tack. Having reached academic heights at the best of America's universities, against her better judgement and my warnings she decided to return home. She has spent the last three years providing much-needed help in our country's social sector. But now she is ready to leave Zambia once more. Not because she doesn't love her job, not because she hasn't helped, but because she, like many other educated Africans who live abroad but are desperate to return home, feels that her country continues to flounder in a seemingly never-ending cycle of corruption, disease, poverty, and aid-dependency. She looks at her situation and asks herself, what is going wrong here?

To be sure, Africa is not one country. It is a continent; a collection of over fifty nations with often vastly different histories, with peoples as disparate as those of North America and southeast Asia, varying lingua francas, and very divergent cultures and religious beliefs.

As a former French colony with Arab influences and a mainly Muslim population, Senegal is quite different from Malawi, a former British colony where Christianity is the dominant religion. And what do lusophone Angola and Mozambique have in common with Ethiopia, which was never colonized? (Ethiopia's defeat of the Italians at the Battle of Adowa, in 1896, meant the country remained, for all intents and purposes, independent until the Italian invasion of 1935.[1])

And economically, besides both being commodity exporters, tea-producing Kenya is structurally quite different from the ex-Belgian colony of the Democratic Republic of Congo, which remains a large mineral exporter with more localized pockets of employment. And the health challenges faced by Ghana (where the prevalence of HIV–AIDS is 2.2 per cent in the population) are undoubtedly quite different from those faced by Swaziland, where reputedly whole villages have been wiped out by the ravages of the disease (prevalence is around 26 per cent of the population – it was almost 40 per cent in 2003).

But there are, sadly, common ties that bind sub-Saharan African countries together. Well-publicized are the degree of poverty, the extent of corruption, the incidence of disease, the dearth of infrastructure, the erratic (but mainly poor) economic showing, political instability, and the historical propensity for violent unrest and even civil war. These are universal themes shared, albeit in varying degrees, across most nations of the African continent. They are the issues that policymakers and governments grapple with each and every day in poverty-stricken Chad, war-torn Somalia, or disease-afflicted Botswana. Whether you are in Zambia, which today has a population of around 10 million people with seventy-two different dialects, or in next-door Zimbabwe, where, with roughly the same population, the indigenous African population can be loosely split into just two large tribal groupings (Shona and Ndebele), Africa's common challenges are real and undeniably stark. Fortunes and misfortunes are intertwined. Even where there are pockets of economic success, it is worth remembering that in the long term no country in Africa can truly exist as an island of prosperity on its own.

For me, finding a sustainable solution to Africa's woes is a personal quest. Having been raised in one of the poorest countries in the world, I feel a strong desire to help families like my own, who continue to suffer the consequences of economic failure every day of their lives. Throughout my professional and academic life as a student of economics I have pondered the question of development. I have often wondered, while other emerging regions have ostensibly turned the corner towards economic prosperity, why my continent has failed. This book is a consequence of my thoughts and deliberations over the years.

This book is written for Africans and African policymakers; and for those in the West and the broader international community who truly wish to see Africa progress. In what follows, I offer my perspective on how we got where we are, and propose ways to find the economic growth which has until now remained elusive.

Although the *Dead Aid* thesis might be controversial, it carries an important message. The lives of billions rest on getting the right financing solutions to the problems of developing nations. After more than five decades of the wrong diagnosis, it is time now to turn the corner and take the harder but indisputably better road. It is the clarion call for change.

Introduction

We live in a culture of aid.

We live in a culture in which those who are better off subscribe – both mentally and financially – to the notion that giving alms to the poor is the right thing to do. In the past fifty years, over US$1 trillion in development-related aid has been transferred from rich countries to Africa. In the past decade alone, on the back of Live 8, Make Poverty History, the Millennium Development Goals, the Millennium Challenge Account, the Africa Commission, and the 2005 G7 meeting (to name a few), millions of dollars each year have been raised in richer countries to support charities working for Africa.

We are made to believe that this is what we ought to be doing. We are accosted on the streets and goaded with pleas on aeroplane journeys; letters flow through our mail boxes and countless television appeals remind us that we have a moral imperative to give more to those who have less. At the 2001 Labour conference, the UK's Prime Minister of the time, Tony Blair, remarked that 'The State of Africa is a scar on the conscience of the world', and that the West should 'provide more aid' as, thus far, amidst the multiple problems facing Africa, the continent had received inadequate amounts of aid.[1]

Deep in every liberal sensibility is a profound sense that in a world of moral uncertainty one idea is sacred, one belief cannot be compromised: the rich should help the poor, and the form of this help should be aid.

The pop culture of aid has bolstered these misconceptions. Aid has become part of the entertainment industry. Media figures, film stars, rock legends eagerly embrace aid, proselytize the need for it, upbraid us for not giving enough, scold governments for not doing enough – and governments respond in kind, fearful of losing popularity and desperate to win favour. Bono attends world summits on aid. Bob Geldof is, to use Tony Blair's own words, 'one of the people that I admire most'. Aid has become a cultural commodity.

Millions march for it.

Governments are judged by it.

But has more than US$1 trillion in development assistance over the last several decades made African people better off? No. In fact, across the globe the recipients of this aid are worse off; much worse off. Aid has helped make the poor poorer, and growth slower. Yet aid remains a centrepiece of today's development policy and one of the biggest ideas of our time.

The notion that aid can alleviate systemic poverty, and has done so, is a myth. Millions in Africa are poorer today because of aid; misery and poverty have not ended but have increased. Aid has been, and continues to be, an unmitigated political, economic, and humanitarian disaster for most parts of the developing world.

How this happened, how the world was gripped with an idea that seemed so right but was in fact so wrong, is what this book is about. *Dead Aid* is the story of the failure of post-war development policy.

Step by step it will dismantle the assumptions and arguments that have supported the single worst decision of modern developmental politics, the choice of aid as the optimum solution to the problem of Africa's poverty. The evidence is as startling as it is obvious. It will contrast countries which have rejected the aid route and prospered with others which have become dependent on aid and been trapped in a vicious circle of corruption, market distortion and further poverty – and thus the 'need' for more aid.

Others before me have criticized aid. But the myth of its effectiveness persists. *Dead Aid* will offer a new model for financing development for the world's poorest countries: one that offers economic growth, promises to significantly reduce African poverty, and most importantly does not rely on aid.

This book is not a counsel of despair. Far from it. The book offers another road; a road less travelled in Africa. Harder, more demanding, more difficult, but in the end the road to growth, prosperity, and independence for the continent. This book is about the aid-free solution to development: why it is right, why it has worked, why it is the only way forward for the world's poorest countries.

PART I

The World of Aid

1. The Myth of Aid

The state of Africa

A decade ago, it was easy to paint a bleak picture of the African continent. Economic prospects were grim, corruption was rampant, social capital was debilitated, tyrannical states were the order of the day, and infrastructure lay in ruins.

Over the past five years, there have been signs that warrant a sliver of optimism. Many African economies have posted annual growth rates around 5 per cent, and a number of countries now host democratic elections.

Three factors are at the core of the African revival.

First, the surge in commodity prices – oil, copper, gold, and foodstuffs – in the last several years has fuelled African exports and increased export revenue. Second, on the back of the market-based policies instituted in the late 1980s, African countries have benefited from a positive policy dividend. This has left Africa's macro-economic fundamentals on the up (growth on the rise, inflation down, more transparent, prudent, and stable monetary and fiscal performance). And despite the news headlines, there have been some noteworthy improvements in social indicators in some countries. In Kenya, for example, HIV prevalence rates have fallen from 15 per cent in 2001 to 6 per cent at the end of 2006.[1] Third, there have been some notable strides in the political landscape across the continent; more than just on paper. For example, of forty-eight sub-Saharan African countries, over 50 per cent hold regular democratic elections that can be deemed free and fair.[2] The occurrence of democratic elections and decline in the levels of perceived corruption in a number of countries (for example, Angola, Ghana, Senegal, Tanzania, Uganda, and, yes, even Nigeria) point to a vastly improved investment climate.

If you simply believe the media headlines, are taken in by the soundbites and quips, you would almost for sure have missed out on some key milestones in Africa's financial development.

Established in 1887, the Johannesburg Stock Exchange is sub-Saharan Africa's oldest stock market. Its opening was followed by Bulawayo's exchange, in what was then the colony of Rhodesia, in 1896, and then Windhoek's, in present-day Namibia, in 1910.[3] Today sixteen African countries boast functioning and transparent stock markets (Botswana, Cameroon, Ghana, Kenya, Malawi, Mauritius, Mozambique, Namibia, Nigeria, South Africa, Swaziland, Rwanda, Tanzania, Uganda, Zambia and Zimbabwe), with market capitalization in 2008 (excluding South Africa) around US$200 billion (around half of the region's GDP).

While it is true that stock market liquidity – the ease with which an investor can buy or sell shares – across most African exchanges is relatively low at an annual turnover ratio of 6 per cent in 2008 (versus an average of 85 per cent in more-developed emerging economies such as Brazil, Russia, India and China), between 2005 and 2006 the growth in liquidity, measured as turnover, was over 50 per cent. All things being equal, liquidity across African markets should markedly improve in the near term.[4]

In three of the past five years African stock exchanges have ranked among the best places to invest, with listed stock returns averaging 40 per cent. Companies like Zambeef (one of Africa's largest agri-businesses, involved in the production, processing, distribution and retailing of beef, chickens, eggs, milk and dairy products) returned 150 per cent in real US$ terms in 2007, and between 2005 and early 2008 the Nigerian banking sector has returned around 300 per cent.

Performance across Africa's bond markets is also impressive. Local debt returned investors 15 per cent in 2006, and 18 per cent in 2007. In the last five years average African credit spreads have collapsed by 250 basis points. What this means is that if a country issues US$100 million in debt, it is saving itself US$2.5 million per year relative to where it was five years ago. And African Private

Equity investments have had a steady record, reputedly yielding around 30 per cent over the past ten years.

But, despite these important recent strides in the macroeconomy and the political landscape, overall the picture in terms of trends in Africa remains a challenging one.

With an average per capita income of roughly US$1 a day, sub-Saharan Africa remains the poorest region in the world.[5] Africa's real per capita income today is lower than in the 1970s, leaving many African countries at least as poor as they were forty years ago. With over half of the 700 million Africans living on less than a dollar a day, sub-Saharan Africa has the highest proportion of poor people in the world – some 50 per cent of the world's poor. And while the number of the world's population and proportion of the world's people in extreme poverty fell after 1980, the proportion of people in sub-Saharan Africa living in abject poverty increased to almost 50 per cent. Between 1981 and 2002, the number of people in the continent living in poverty nearly doubled, leaving the average African poorer today than just two decades ago. And looking ahead, the 2007 United Nations Human Development Report forecasts that sub-Saharan Africa will account for almost one third of world poverty in 2015, up from one fifth in 1990 (this largely due to the dramatic developmental strides being made elsewhere around the emerging world).

Life expectancy has stagnated – Africa is the only continent where life expectancy is less than sixty years; today it hovers around fifty years, and in some countries it has fallen back to what it was in the 1950s (life expectancy in Swaziland is a paltry thirty years). The decrease in life expectancy is mainly attributed to the rise of the HIV–AIDS pandemic. One in seven children across the African continent die before the age of five.[6] These statistics are particularly worrying in that (as with many other developing regions of the world), roughly 50 per cent of Africa's population is young – below the age of fifteen years.

Adult literacy across most African countries has plummeted below pre-1980 levels. Literacy rates, health indicators (malaria, water-borne diseases such as bilharzia and cholera) and income inequality all remain a cause for worry. And still across important indicators, the trend in Africa is not just downwards: Africa is (negatively) decoupling from the progress being made across the rest of the world. Even with African growth rates averaging 5 per cent a year over the past several years, the Africa Progress Panel pointed out in 2007 that growth is still short of the 7 per cent that needs to be sustained to make substantial inroads into poverty reduction.[7]

On the political side, some 50 per cent of the continent remains under non-democratic rule. According to the Polity IV database, Africa is still home to at least eleven fully autocratic regimes (Congo-Brazzaville, Equatorial Guinea, Eritrea, Gabon, The Gambia, Mauritania, Rwanda, Sudan, Swaziland, Uganda and Zimbabwe). Three African heads of state (dos Santos of Angola, Obiang of Equatorial Guinea and Bongo of Gabon) have been in power since the 1970s (having ascended to power on 2 December 1967, President Bongo has recently celebrated his fortieth year in power). Five other presidents have had a lock on power since the 1980s (Compaore of Burkina Faso, Biya of Cameroon, Conte of Guinea, Museveni of Uganda and Mugabe of Zimbabwe). Since 1996, eleven countries have been embroiled in civil wars (Angola, Burundi, Chad, Democratic Republic of Congo, Republic of Congo, Guinea Bissau, Liberia, Rwanda, Sierra Leone, Sudan and Uganda).[8] And according to the May 2008 annual Global Peace Index, out of the ten bottom countries four African states are among the least peaceful in the world (in order, Central African Republic, Chad, Sudan and Somalia) – the most of any one continent.

Why is it that Africa, alone among the continents of the world, seems to be locked into a cycle of dysfunction? Why is it that out of all the continents in the world Africa seems unable to convincingly get its foot on the economic ladder? Why in a recent survey did seven out of the top ten 'failed states' hail from that continent? Are Africa's people universally more incapable? Are its leaders genetically more venal, more ruthless, more corrupt? Its policy-makers more innately feckless? What is it about Africa that holds it back, that seems to render it incapable of joining the rest of the globe in the twenty-first century?

The answer has its roots in aid.

What is aid?

Broadly speaking there exist three types of aid: humanitarian or emergency aid, which is mobilized and dispensed in response to catastrophes and calamities – for example, aid in response to the 2004 Asian tsunami, or monies which targeted the cyclone-hit Myanmar in 2008; charity-based aid, which is disbursed by charitable organizations to institutions or people on the ground; and systematic aid – that is, aid payments made directly to governments either through government-to-government transfers (in which case it is termed bilateral aid) or transferred via institutions such as the World Bank (known as multilateral aid).

While there are obvious and fundamental merits to emergency aid, criticisms can be levelled against it as well as against charitable giving. Charities are often criticized, with some justification, for poor implementation, high administrative costs and the fact that they are on occasion coerced to do their donor government's bidding – despite the obvious lack of relevance to a local context. For example, in 2005, the United States pledged US$15 billion over five years to fight AIDS (mainly through the President's Emergency Plan for AIDS Relief (PEPFAR) launched in January 2003).[9] But this had strings attached. Two thirds of the money had to go to pro-abstinence programmes, and would not be available to any organizations with clinics that offered abortion services or even counselling. And nine months after the 2004 Asian tsunami, for whatever the reason (bureaucracy, institutional inefficiencies or the absence of suitable organizations on the ground to disburse the monies), the charity World Vision had spent less than a quarter of the US$100 million it had raised.

But this book is not concerned with emergency and charity-based aid. The significant sums of this type of aid that flow to

Africa simply disguise the fundamental (yet erroneous) mindset that pervades the West – that aid, whatever its form, is a good thing. Besides, charity and emergency aid are small beer when compared with the billions transferred each year directly to poor countries' governments.

Large systematic cash transfers from rich countries to African governments have tended to be in the form of concessional loans (that is, money lent at below market interest rates, and often for much longer lending periods than ordinary commercial markets) or grants (which is essentially money given for nothing in return).

There is a school of thought which argues that recipient countries view loans, which carry the burden of future repayment, as different from grants. That the prospects of repayment mean loans induce governments to use funds wisely and to mobilize taxes and maintain current levels of revenue collection. Whereas grants are viewed as free resources and could therefore perfectly substitute for a government's domestic revenues.

This distinction has led many donors to push for a policy of grants instead of loans to poor countries. The logic is that much of the investment that poor countries need to make has a long gestation period before it starts to produce the kinds of changes in GDP growth that will yield the tax revenues needed to service loans. Indeed, many scholars have argued that it was precisely because many African countries have, over time, received (floating rate) loans, and not grants, to finance public investments that they became so heavily indebted, and that aid has not helped them reach their development objectives.

Yet ultimately the question becomes how strongly recipient governments perceive loans as being different from grants. If a large share of foreign loans are provided on highly concessional terms, and loans are frequently forgiven, policymakers in poor economies may come to view them as roughly equivalent to grants, and as such the distinction between (aid) loans and grants as practically irrelevant. Over recent decades, the pattern of aid to Africa seems to gel with this view of the world – one in which loans are not seen as distinct from grants.

Therefore, for the purposes of this book, aid is defined as the sum total of both concessional loans and grants. It is these billions that have hampered, stifled and retarded Africa's development. And it is these billions that *Dead Aid* will address.

2. A Brief History of Aid

The tale of aid begins in earnest in the first three weeks of July 1944, at a meeting held at the Mount Washington Hotel in Bretton Woods, New Hampshire, USA. Against the backdrop of the Second World War, over 700 delegates from some forty-four countries resolved to establish a framework for a global system of financial and monetary management.[1] As discussed later, it is from this gathering that the dominant framework of aid–infused development would emerge.

The origins of large-scale aid transfers date as far back as the nineteenth century – when even in 1896 the US provided overseas assistance in the form of food aid. Under the Colonial Development Act of 1929, the British government administered grants for infrastructure projects across poorer countries. Aid transfers in these early periods were as much about donor largesse as they were about political control over the colonial domain, and only later, in the 1940 British Colonial Development and Welfare Act, was the programme expanded to allow funding of social sector activities.

Post-war aid can be broken down into seven broad categories: its birth at Bretton Woods in the 1940s; the era of the Marshall Plan in the 1950s; the decade of industrialization of the 1960s; the shift towards aid as an answer to poverty in the 1970s; aid as the tool for stabilization and structural adjustment in the 1980s; aid as a buttress of democracy and governance in the 1990s; culminating in the present-day obsession with aid as the only solution to Africa's myriad of problems.

The main agenda of the Bretton Woods conference was to restructure international finance, establish a multilateral trading system and construct a framework for economic cooperation that would avoid a repeat of the Great Depression of the 1930s. As they anticipated the post-Second World War era, the architects of the

1944 Bretton Woods gathering foresaw that if Europe were to regain any semblance of social, political or economic stability, vast injections of aid would have to be poured in. There was a clear recognition that in the post-war period the fractured nations of Europe would need a massive cash injection to spur a return to their previous levels of development. Damaged though Europe was, this money was (fortuitously) going into already existing physical, legal and social infrastructures which simply needed fixing.

John Maynard Keynes, the pre-eminent British economist, and Harry Dexter White, at that time the US Secretary of State, led the discussions which laid the foundations for three organizations: the International Bank for Reconstruction and Development (commonly known as the World Bank), the International Monetary Fund (IMF) and the International Trade Organization.

At the time of their inception, the exact responsibilities of the World Bank and the IMF were clearly delineated. In very broad terms, the World Bank was designed to facilitate capital investment for reconstruction, and in the aftermath of the war the IMF was to manage the global financial system. In later years, both institutions would come to occupy centre-stage in the development discourse, but the original mandate targeted reconstruction, rather than development per se.

At its core, the reconstruction agenda assumed that the demands on post-war investment could not be met without some adequate means of pooling the investment risk between countries. There was wide acknowledgement that few countries would be able to fulfil the role of foreign lender; and the basic principle of the World Bank was that no matter what country actually did the foreign lending, all member nations should participate in underwriting the risk involved. Early financial transfers from international institutions included a US$250 million reconstruction loan to France signed on 9 May 1946, followed by reconstruction loans to the Netherlands, Denmark and Luxembourg in August 1947. These aid transfers were undoubtedly at the heart of the reconstruction process that almost certainly contributed to the economic power-house that Europe has become today.

Alongside the World Bank, the IMF was mandated with the specific responsibility of promoting the stability of the world economy. At the time it began operations on 1 March 1947, the IMF was charged with promoting and supervising international monetary cooperation amongst countries, and thus forestalling any possible global financial crisis. By the end of the 1940s an aid-led economic framework was firmly in place, but it was not until later in the decade that the first large-scale government-to-government aid transfer occurred.

On 5 June 1947, at Harvard University, the US Secretary of State, George C. Marshall, outlined a radical proposal by which America would provide a rescue package of up to US$20 billion (over US$100 billion in today's terms) for a ravaged Europe.[2] As Europe emerged from the devastation of the Second World War with little to sell for hard currency, and experiencing one of the worst winters on record, General Marshall argued for an aggressive financial intervention by the United States. In return, European governments would draw up an economic revival plan.

Under the Marshall Plan, the United States embarked on an aid programme to fourteen European countries which saw the transfer of assistance worth roughly US$13 billion throughout the five-year life of the plan from 1948 to 1952. Among the top five aid recipients from the Marshall Plan were Great Britain, which received the lion's share of 24 per cent, and France, Italy and Germany, which received 20, 11 and 10 per cent, respectively. In per capita terms smaller European countries received more support: Norway received US$136 per person, Austria US$131, Greece US$128 and the Netherlands US$111.

The idea that the Marshall Plan is hailed as a success has remained, to a large extent, unquestioned. The plan was clearly successful in bringing Western Europe back onto a strong economic footing, providing the US with the vehicle to influence foreign policy, winning it allies in Western Europe and building a solid foundation for US-led multilateralism. Aid had restored broken infrastructure. Aid had brought political stability, restored hope and not only given a future to defeated peoples, to bankrupt nations and to broken lands, but also benefited the donor nation itself, keeping the US economy afloat while the world around it had crumbled.

More importantly, if aid worked in Europe, if it gave to Europe what Europe needed, why couldn't it do the same everywhere else? By the end of the 1950s, once reconstruction in Europe was seen to be working, attention turned towards other parts of the world, and specifically, in the context of aid, Africa.

Africa was ripe for aid. The continent was characterized by a largely uneducated population, low-salaried employment, a virtually non-existent tax base, poor access to global markets and derelict infrastructure. Armed with the ideas and experience of the Marshall Plan, richer countries saw Africa as a prime target for aid. So aid began to appear.

As the US funnelled large sums to Europe through the Marshall plan, World Bank and IMF resources were freed up. Monies that had been earmarked by the Bretton Woods institutions for post-war European reconstruction could now be directed towards the emerging (African) development agenda.

Perhaps more crucially for the aid-based agenda that ensued, it was widely assumed that poor countries lacked the financial capital to spur development. In the wake of the Marshall Plan success, it became a widely accepted view that investment capital was critical for economic growth. In the absence of any significant domestic savings and lacking the physical and human capital to attract private investment, foreign aid was seen as the only way to trigger higher investment, which would thus lead to higher economic growth. As far as policymakers could see, there was no obvious alternative.

There were of course other reasons why Britain, America and to a lesser extent France turned their attention to Africa. By the mid-1950s Africa was undergoing profound changes – with Western powers loosening the chains of colonialism, many countries were gaining their independence. Countries such as Ghana in 1957, Kenya in 1963, and Malawi and Zambia in 1964 broke from the colonial fold to become independent states between 1956 and 1966; in all, thirty-one African countries did so. Independent they may have been on paper, but independence dependent on the financial largesse of their former colonial masters was the reality. For the West, aid became a means by which Britain and France combined their new-found altruism with a hefty dollop of self-interest – maintaining strategic geopolitical holds. For the US, aid became the tool of another political contest – the Cold War.

While the Cold War was peppered with outbreaks of physical hostility (for example, in Korea), much of the battle for world hegemony between the US and the USSR was fought economic-ally and on foreign soil. The choice of weapon – aid. Africa saw many such battles. Aid became the key tool in the contest to turn the world capitalist or communist. The Soviet Union was, of course, a staunch supporter (and financier) of some of Africa's greatest communists – Patrice Lumumba in Congo and Mengistu Haile Mariam in Ethiopia. And the US, by contrast, rewarded its supporters, such as Zaire's Mobutu Sese Seko.

As such, the aid imperative took on an added dimension: not how deserving a country might be or the nature of its leadership, but rather the willingness of a desperately impoverished country to ally itself with one camp or another – benevolent leader or vicious tyrant, as long as they were onside, what did it matter?

It is impossible to know for sure what the true motivations for granting foreign aid to Africa were, but granted it was.

The 1960s: the decade of industrialization

By the beginning of the 1960s some US$100 million in aid had been transferred to the African continent. This was a mere trickle compared to the avalanche of billions of dollars of aid that would eventually make its way to Africa.

The early part of the 1960s also saw the underlying shift towards a greater focus on aid funding for large-scale industrial projects. The prevailing view was that because these projects had longer-term pay-offs (for example, the funding of infrastructure projects such as roads and railways), they were unlikely to be funded by the private sector. One such example is the double-curvature, hydro-electric, concrete arch Kariba dam that straddles the border be-tween Zambia and Zimbabwe; it was built throughout the decade. The dam, whose construction began under British colonial rule in the mid-1950s, was finally completed at a cost of US$480 million in 1977. Today it still ranks as one of the largest dams in the world.

By 1965, when around half of sub-Saharan Africa's roughly fifty states were independent, aid had already reached at least US$950 million. Ghana, which had won its independence from Britain in 1957, had received as much as US$90 million in aid flows. Zambia, Kenya and Malawi, all independent by 1964 had, on average, received about US$315 million each by the end of the decade. Statistical records from the 1960s are scant, and estimates of the miles of tarred road and railway track, the numbers of bridges and airports, that aid helped build remain unclear. As such, the true value of the surfeit of aid that had gone to Africa remains open to debate, but by the beginning of the 1970s there was still not much infrastructure to speak of.

The foreign aid agenda of the 1970s: the shift to a poverty focus

On 17 October 1973, Arab states placed an embargo on oil as a retaliation for US support for Israel in the Yom Kippur War. In just a few months, the price of petrol quadrupled, sending the global economy into turmoil. As oil prices soared, oil-exporting countries deposited the additional cash with international banks, which in turn eagerly sought to lend this money to the developing world. Lax economic and financial policies (for example, the low amounts central banks required commercial banks to keep in reserve) meant that the volume of lending to even the poorest and most un-creditworthy countries around the world was enormous. The wall of freely supplied money led to extremely low, and even negative, real interest rates, and encouraged many poorer

economies to start borrowing even more in order to repay previous
debts.

In Africa, as oil prices rose many countries saw food prices
rocket and recession take hold. In 1975 Ghana's GDP contracted
by 12 per cent, inflation rose from 3 per cent in 1970 to 30 per
cent in 1975, and shot to 116 per cent in 1977. In Congo-Kinshasa,
inflation rose from 8 per cent in 1970 to 80 per cent in 1976,
and reached 101 per cent in 1979. Almost inevitably, food and
commodity price shocks fuelled by rises in oil prices led to the
shift towards a more poverty-based approach to development.

Under Robert McNamara, the World Bank very publicly reori-
ented its strategies towards this more pronounced poverty focus.
Donor countries followed suit: in 1975 the UK published its white
paper *More Aid for the Poorest* and in the same year the US passed
the International Development and Food Assistance Act, which
stipulated that 75 per cent of its Food for Peace Program would
go to countries with a per capita income of less than US$300.

In practical terms this meant redirecting aid away from large
infrastructure investment (power, transport, etc.), and towards
projects in agriculture and rural development, social services
(including housing, education and health), mass inoculation programmes, adult literacy campaigns, as well as food for the mal-
nourished. The emphasis was now on the poor. By the end of the
1970s the proportion of aid allocated to social services had crept
to over 50 per cent, up from under 10 per cent in the previous
decade.

Although in the mid-1970s nearly two thirds of aid was for
infrastructure – roads, railways, water and sewerage, ports, airports, power stations and telecommunications, the proportion of
poverty-oriented lending rose from 5 per cent in the late 1970s to
50 per cent by the early 1980s. In the year of the first oil spike
(between 1973 and 1974) the volume of poverty-related aid flows
increased threefold; it more than doubled at the time of the second
oil jump between 1979 and 1980. It should be understood that,
like the majority of the infrastructure aid, much of the poverty-
related aid did not come for free. Aid costs money. And unless it's

in the form of grants, it has to be paid back, with interest. This point would later come back to haunt many African states.

By the beginning of the 1970s the growth-oriented strategy was widely believed in policy circles to have failed in its mission to deliver sustained economic growth. Mounting numbers of people living in a state of absolute poverty, increasing levels of unemployment, rising income inequality, worsening balance of trade positions and a growing sense that sustained growth – real sustained growth – could not occur without materially improving the livelihood of society's poor demanded a new aid strategy.

Yet, despite the aid aimed at poverty alleviation, recipients under the programme in countries such as Zambia would later see their poverty levels skyrocket and growth rates plummet. Another shift was underway in the 1970s. Up until the early part of the decade the US government (under the auspices of the US Agency for International Development) had disbursed the largest amount of aid to the developing world. This changed under Robert McNamara's presidency of the World Bank, and after its 1973 annual meeting the World Bank became the largest aid donor.

The foreign aid agenda of the 1980s: the lost age of development

By the end of the 1970s Africa was awash with aid. In total, the continent had amassed around US$36 *billion* in foreign assistance. With the commodity boom creditors were only too happy to provide loans. Although economic pressures and financial instability had been largely contained after the 1973 oil crisis, come the 1979 oil spike precipitated by the Iran–Iraq war, it was a different story.

Foreign money had been flowing not only to Africa, but all across the world. Throughout the 1960s and 1970s Latin American countries borrowed vast sums of money, also to finance their burgeoning economies. Between 1975 and 1982, for example, Latin American debt to commercial banks increased at a cumulative annual rate of 20.4 per cent. This heightened borrowing led Latin America to quadruple its external debt from US$75 billion in 1975 to more than US$315 billion in 1983, or 50 per cent of the region's GDP.

The 1979 oil crisis produced financial pressures of insurmountable proportions, and the official policy response did not help. The policy reaction, particularly by major economies such as the US and UK, differed drastically from the earlier approach of simply dumping in more aid to stave off the impact on the poor. Central bankers in the industrialized world reacted to the second price shock and fears of mounting inflation by tightening monetary policy – that is, mainly raising interest rates. Most of the bank loans to developing countries were based on floating interest rates, so as policymakers raised interest rates, so too the cost of borrowing increased – often to levels where debt was unsustainable.

Africa's debt service (interest payments and the repayment of principal) reached around US$8 billion in 1982, up from US$2 billion in 1975. Almost inevitably, the environment of higher international interest rates led to worldwide recession and, in turn, less demand for developing countries' exports, and hence lower foreign exchange earnings. Eventually, as emerging countries were unable to service their accumulated debts there was only one alternative.

On 12 August 1982 Mexico's Secretary of Finance telephoned the US Federal Reserve Chairman, the US Secretary of the Treasury and the IMF's Managing Director to inform them that Mexico would be unable to meet its 16 August debt obligations to its bank creditors. Other countries soon followed suit. In Africa alone, some eleven countries – Angola, Cameroon, Congo, Ivory Coast, Gabon, The Gambia, Mozambique, Niger, Nigeria, Tanzania, and Zambia – defaulted on their obligations.[3]

The debt crisis threatened to undermine the very foundations of global financial stability. If emerging nations were allowed to default unchecked, this would have led to a complete collapse of the international financial structure. The survival of international creditors, such as banks, who relied on getting paid back for the loans was in jeopardy. Much like the risks surrounding the 2008 sub-prime credit crisis, this could have resulted in a catastrophic run on the banks, a global financial meltdown and all that it entails – unemployment, galloping inflation and economic depression.

The solution to the crisis was to restructure the debt. Thus the IMF formed the Structural Adjustment Facility – latterly, the Enhanced Structural Adjustment Facility – specifically to lend money to defaulting nations to help them repay what they owed. Necessary though this was, the end result only served to increase poor countries' aid-dependence and put them deeper into debt.

This intervention was called a restructuring, but in reality it was merely a reincarnation of the aid model. Invariably, because international private lending markets dried up and as commercial banks were no longer willing to lend to poor countries, the Bretton Woods institutions would reclaim their central position as chief lenders to emerging economies.

From the high hopes and ambitions of their early independence, many African countries had been reduced to a state of near destitution and renewed dependency. Facing falling income from trade (prices of commodities such as oil and sugar had retreated to historically low levels: oil fell from US$38 a barrel in 1980 to US$15.10 in 1986 (a 60 per cent drop in just four years), and sugar from 65 cents per pound to a low of just under 7 cents per pound in 1978), weighed down by enormous debt burdens, high interest rates and declining demand for their goods, it was difficult to see what, if anything, had been achieved in the preceding twenty years. But amidst this financial chaos around the world, another fundamental shift in economic thinking was occurring; one which would again have implications for aid.

Up until the 1980s the notion that governments were the ultimate arbiter of resource allocation lay at the core of economic planning, leaving little room for any sort of private sector. Government-led economic planning had appeared to work well in the Soviet Union, and many Western governments were keen to avert another great depression by cementing their influence in economic management. Socialist policies that had placed government at the centre of economic activity and nationalized much of private industry were believed to be the fastest route to economic prosperity. This was true across the developed world – for example, in Britain and France well before the 1980s – as well as in many African countries in the post-independence period.

By the 1980s, however, there was a growing sense among leading policymakers that there were inherent structural impediments to the functioning of economic markets. Far from being a catalyst for development, excessive government involvement was viewed as the prime obstacle to growth; rather than facilitating healthy economic expansion, it was the source of economic distortion.

The 1980s also saw the rise of the neo-liberal thinking which argued that governments should liberalize their economies in favour of the laissez-faire paradigm, which encompassed (and indeed acknowledged the importance of) the private market. The experience of the newly industrializing economies of Asia gave these market-based ideas a popularity boost in policy circles in the United States and Europe. The Asian tigers seemed to have achieved high growth rates and unprecedented poverty reduction with free-market policies and an outward orientation. As free-market proponents, Milton Friedman and the Chicago School of Economics had great influence on the policies and thinking of the US President, Ronald Reagan, and the UK's Prime Minister, Margaret Thatcher. The policies that ensued (Reaganomics and Thatcherism) bore all the hallmarks of an economic revolution, and there was little room for compromise; so too in Africa, where these free-market polices were packaged and sold as the new development agenda.

In Africa, as with other parts of the developing world, this economic overhaul necessitated two new aid-based programmes: first, stabilization, and then structural adjustment. Stabilization meant reducing a country's imbalances to reasonable levels – for example, the government's fiscal position and the country's import–export ratio. Meanwhile structural adjustment was aimed at encouraging greater trade liberalization and reducing price and structural rigidities by such means as removing subsidies.

Both the World Bank and the IMF launched aggressive aid programmes to institute these two initiatives; the IMF's Structural Adjustment and Enhanced Structural Adjustment Facilities are examples of these. Poor governments received cash in the form of budgetary support, and in return agreed to embrace the free-market solutions to development. This would entail minimizing the role of the state, privatizing previously nationalized industries, liberalizing trade and dramatically reducing the civil service. Between 1986 and 1996, for example, six African countries – Benin, the Central African Republic, Guinea, Madagascar, Mali and Uganda – shed more than 10 per cent of their civil service workforce.[4] The privatization of African state-owned enterprises across all sectors (no sector sacred – manufacturing and industry, agriculture, tourism, services, trade, transport, financial, energy, mining, water, electricity and telecommunications) meant the government stake of corporate equity fell from almost 90 per cent to just 10 per cent ownership in six years. The free markets gave African economies the freedom to succeed, but also the freedom to fail. In Zambia, for instance, an aggressive privatization programme saw the closure of the country's national airline carrier, Zambia Airways.[5]

From the start of the debt crisis in 1982, IMF flows rose from US$8 billion to US$12 billion in 1983. With the onset and resolution of the debt crisis in the 1980s, poverty-related aid flows subsided, tilting in favour of stabilization and structural adjustment packages (together known as programme aid). Since the 1980s the World Bank's share of adjustment-related lending has averaged between 20 and 25 per cent of its total disbursements. During the 1980s bilateral flows also became more concessional in nature and by the early 1990s over 90 per cent were grants.

Alongside rising government-to-government transfers (bilateral aid), multilateral institutions continued their aggressive march towards gaining greater importance – both in terms of the volume of aid disbursed and as architects of development policy. By 1989, the Washington Consensus (a standard reform package of economic policy prescriptions, mainly on monetary and fiscal policy for the countries most affected by economic crisis) became the backbone of the development strategy pursued by the Washington DC-based institutions (the IMF, World Bank, and US Treasury Department).

The foreign aid agenda of the 1990s: a question of governance

By the end of the 1980s, emerging-market countries' debt was at least US$1 trillion, and the cost of servicing these obligations colossal. Indeed, the cost became so substantial that it eventually dwarfed foreign aid going into poor countries – leading to a net reverse flow from poor countries to rich to the tune of US$15 billion every year between 1987 and 1989. From a development point of view, this was absurd. Were it not for the tragic consequences, it would be farcical. Africa's economic growth had been in a steady decline, poverty levels were on the rise and the stench of rampant corruption was growing ever more pungent. (After his meeting with President Reagan, Zaire's President Mobutu Sese Seko had asked for easier terms to service the country's US$5 billion debt; he then promptly leased Concorde to fly his daughter to her wedding in the Ivory Coast.[6]

This backdrop, seen by many as the spectacular crash of the aid-based development model, set the tone for the policy shifts of much of the 1990s. Having seen the failure of fifty years of competing aid interventions, donors now laid the blame for Africa's economic woes at the door of political leadership and weak institutions.

While much of Asia and Latin America was firmly back on a growth path, with issues of economic instability behind it, many African countries stagnated, and in some of the worst cases economically regressed.

It was around this time that the donor community converged on the idea that governance – good governance, needed for sustainable economic growth – was lacking across much of sub-Saharan Africa. Good governance was a euphemism for strong and credible institutions, transparent rule of law and economies free of rampant corruption. Also around this time, geopolitically, the world had been undergoing a transformation of its own, a transformation that would have far-reaching implications for Africa and the aid agenda for the continent.

Throughout the latter half of the twentieth century and up until the 1990s, the Cold War had provided richer countries with the political imperative to give aid monies even to the most corrupt and venal despots in Africa. One of the features of the Cold War was the West's ability and eagerness to support, bankroll and prop up a swathe of pathological and downright dangerous dictators. From Idi Amin in the east, to Mobutu Sese Seko in the west, from Ethiopia's Mengistu to Liberia's Samuel Doe, the competition among these leaders to be more brutal to their people, more spendthrift, more indifferent to their country's needs than their neighbours were, was matched only by the willingness of international donors to give them the money to realize their dreams. Bokassa's coronation as Emperor of the Central African Empire in 1977 alone cost US$22 million.[7] Across many African states, corruption was running at epidemic levels. In 1996, among fifty-four countries around the world, Nigeria was ranked the most corrupt nation, scoring a dismal 0.69 out of 10 on corruption rankings.[8]

Despite this corrupt environment, everyone continued to lend. In answer to mounting criticism of raging crooked, shady and fraudulent practices, donors offered qualifications. For example, the World Bank pledged continued aid support, with the proviso that aid monies must also target governance reform, with the aim of improving the civil service and government bureaucracy (through teaching skills, transparency and institutional reform).

Governance remains at the heart of aid today. Whether this aid strategy has any long-term effects, however, remains an open question. Have Africans been trained in ethics and good governance at Western universities? Yes. Have radical reforms aimed at improving transparency and efficiency been implemented? Yes, at least on paper. But it is debatable whether these initiatives have any real bite in countries which still opt to be dependent on aid.

Alongside governance emerged the West's growing obsession with democracy for the developing world. The installation of democracy was the donor's final refuge; the last-ditch attempt to show that aid interventions could work, would work, if only the political conditions were right. The 1960s' growth agenda had failed to deliver growth and reduce poverty; as had the 1970s' emphasis on the poor, and the 1980s' focus on economic stabilization and adjustment. So after three decades of aid-centric development models, it was left to Western democracy to save the day. In its essence, democracy was perceived to be the way in which countries could grow and develop; and if the democratic ethos and institutions were transplanted to African states, then these countries would finally begin to prosper. Democracy was the ultimate key.

Democracy, real liberal democracy, means political representatives are chosen through elections that are open, free and fair; where virtually all adults possess the right to vote; where civil and political liberties are broadly protected; and where elected authorities are not subject to the tutelary control of military or clerical leaders. For the West, the process of open and fair elections had taken centuries to evolve, but the hope was that (coupled with aid) shoe-horning democracy into underdeveloped nations would guarantee that African countries would see a sudden change in their economic and political fortunes. Yet, as discussed later, it would soon become clear that any improvements in Africa's economic profile have been largely achieved in spite of (nominal) democracy, not because of it.[9]

By the end of the Cold War in 1991, the USSR was no longer a tangible threat, and China had not yet appeared as a protagonist in Africa's development story. So whereas in the past the aid policy had, to a great extent, been governed by Cold War demands, Western donors were now no longer bound by such political considerations. The Soviet Union had, on average, disbursed US$300 million a year to Africa (58 per cent went to Ethiopia), but after the break-up of the union this amount would almost certainly have fallen considerably. Donors could now pick and choose, when, why and to whom they doled out aid – if at all.

Where foreign aid is concerned, the 1990s were characterized by two themes. First, there was the dominance of multilateral agencies, such as the World Bank and the United Nations Development Programme (UNDP), as the leading aid donors; their share of multilateral giving rose from 23 per cent in the 1970s to 30 per cent in the early 1990s. Much of the official flow of aid was on a concessional basis, with grants constituting more than 90 per cent of total official assistance by 1996 – up from 60 per cent twenty years earlier.

Second, there was the onset of donor fatigue in the latter part of the decade. With the geopolitical rationale for giving aid gone, the amount of aid to Africa dwindled dramatically. In the early 1990s, official donor aid (excluding emergency aid and debt relief) to Africa averaged US$15 billion a year, compared to around US$5 billion a year in the 1970s. Having accounted for more than 60 per cent on average of total cash to the continent (net disbursements) during the 1987–92 period (peaking in 1990 at 70 per cent), the share of official foreign aid steadily declined to a little more than 30 per cent of disbursements between 1993 and 1997. Similarly the net official development assistance (ODA – the donors' term for official aid) disbursements as a share of donor GNP fell from 0.38 per cent in 1982 to 0.22 per cent in 1997. For many developing countries (mainly in Asia and Latin America) private flows had largely replaced aid flows, rising from 26 per cent in 1987–92 to 55 per cent in 1993–7.

However, unlike other emerging zones, sub-Saharan Africa did not witness a concomitant rise in private capital inflows as aid flows declined. Despite the decline in net aid flows to Africa over the 1990s, net disbursements at the end of the period were still larger than in 1987, and, furthermore, foreign aid continued (and continues to this day) to be the predominant source of financial resources for much of the continent. In some cases in Africa, aid still represented as much as 90 per cent of net disbursements between 1987 and 1996.

So there had been a marked upward trend in the real value of foreign assistance from the 1960s; this peaked in 1992, and since then aid volumes have fallen. Africa's total net ODA has declined from a high of US$17 billion to US$12 billion in 1999.

During the 1990s another view was also emerging about Africa's failure to develop. Aside from an absence of quality governance and of free and fair democratic process, and the emergence of endemic corruption, there was a sense from some quarters that if only Africa could be released from its yoke of debt in one fell swoop, it could finally achieve that elusive goal – economic prosperity. It was debt that was holding Africa back. And in that sense it was the West's fault, as it was the West to whom Africa owed billions. Morality – Western, liberal, guilt-tripped morality – seeped into the development equation. Soon everyone would join in.

The foreign aid agenda of the 2000s: the rise of glamour aid

In 2000, Africa became the focus of orchestrated world-wide pity, and not for the first time. The Nigerian humanitarian catastrophe of Biafra in 1971 (the same year as the Beatle George Harrison's Concert for Bangladesh) had demanded that the world respond to human catastrophe. Consciousness was raised several notches with Bob Geldof's 13 July 1985 Live Aid Concert where, with 1.5 billion people watching, public discourse became a public disco.

Live Aid had not only been triumphant in bringing Africa's plight to the wider public; it also trumpeted an era of morality. In the run-up to the new millennium, crusades like the Jubilee Debt Campaign capitalized on people's desperate desire to be a part of something that would give aid and development policy another dimension. African leaders such as Tanzania's President Mkapa later encapsulated the feeling of the day in his speech at the Jubilee Debt Campaign Conference in February 2005, calling it a 'scandal that we are forced to choose between basic health and education for our people and repaying historical debt'.

Thus, the way was paved for the army of moral campaigners – the pop stars, the movie stars, new philanthropists and even Pope John Paul II – to carve out niches for themselves, as they took on the fight for more, not less, aid to be sent to Africa, even after billions of dollars of debt were cancelled – in essence, cancelling debt on the one hand, and replacing it with a swathe of new aid, and thus the prospect of fresh debt all over again, with the other. The aid campaigners capitalized on the success of raising cash for emergency aid, and extended it to a platform to raise development aid; something entirely different.

In more recent times, the Irish musician Bono has made his case directly to the US President, George Bush, in a White House visit in October 2005, and Bob Geldof was a guest at the 2005 G8 meeting in Gleneagles, Scotland, and advised the UK's Commission to Africa. It would appear, despondent with their record of failure, that Western donors are increasingly looking to anyone for guidance on how best to tackle Africa's predicament.

Scarcely does one see Africa's (elected) officials or those African policymakers charged with the development portfolio offer an opinion on what should be done, or what might actually work to save the continent from its regression. This very important responsibility has, for all intents and purposes, and to the bewilderment and chagrin of many an African, been left to musicians who reside outside Africa. One disastrous consequence of this has been that honest, critical and serious dialogue and debate on the merits and demerits of aid have atrophied. As one critic of the aid model remarked, 'my voice can't compete with an electric guitar'.

At the end of it all, it is virtually impossible to draw on Africa's aid-led development experience and argue that aid has worked. The broadest consequences of the aid model have been ruinous. Rwanda's President Paul Kagame put it most simply: 'The primary reason [that there is little to show for the more than US$300 billion of aid that has gone to Africa since 1970] is that in the context of post-Second World War geopolitical and strategic rivalries and economic interests, much of this aid was spent on creating and sustaining client regimes of one type or another, with minimal regard to developmental outcomes on our continent.'[10]

Donors, development agencies and policymakers have, by and large, chosen to ignore the blatant alarm signals, and have continued to pursue the aid-based model even when it has become apparent that aid, under whatever guise, is not working. Even when aid has not been stolen, it has been unproductive. The proof of the pudding is in the eating, and ever so clearly the preponderance of evidence is on this side. Given Africa's current economic state it is hard to see how any growth registered is a direct result of aid. If anything, the evidence of the last fifty years points to the reverse – slower growth, higher poverty and Africa left off the economic ladder.

We meant well

More than US$2 trillion of foreign aid has been transferred from rich countries to poor over the past fifty years – Africa the biggest recipient, by far. Yet regardless of the motivation for aid-giving – economic, political or moral – aid has failed to deliver the promise of sustainable economic growth and poverty reduction. At every turn of the development tale of the last five decades, policymakers have chosen to maintain the status quo and furnish Africa with more aid.

Aid has not lived up to expectations. It remains at the heart of the development agenda, despite the fact that there are very compelling reasons to show that it perpetuates the cycle of poverty and derails sustainable economic growth. Paul Kagame rightly also laments that 'While more than US$300 billion in aid has apparently been disbursed to our continent since 1970, there is little to show for it in terms of economic growth and human development.'[11]

Aid is not working. And here's why.

3. Aid is Not Working

Consider this: in the past forty years at least a dozen developing countries have experienced phenomenal economic growth. Many of these, mostly Asian, countries have grown by almost 10 per cent of GDP per year, surpassing the growth rates of leading industrialized economies, and significantly reducing poverty. In some instances, poorer countries have leap-frogged the per capita income levels of leading developed economies, and this trend is set to continue: by some estimates, star emerging-market performers such as Brazil, Russia, India and China are projected to exceed the economic growth rates of nearly all industrialized economies by the year 2050. Yet, over the same period, as many as thirty other developing countries, mainly aid-dependent in sub-Saharan Africa, have failed to generate consistent economic growth, and have even regressed.

Many reasons have been offered to account for why African countries are not working: in particular, geographical, historical, cultural, tribal and institutional. While each of them is convincing in explaining Africa's poor showing, they do not tell the whole story.

One argument, advanced by geographical determinists such as Jared Diamond in *Guns, Germs and Steel* (1997), is that a country's wealth and success depend on its geographical environment and topography. Certain environments are easier to manipulate than others and, as such, societies that can domesticate plants and animals with relative ease are likely to be more prosperous. At a minimum, a country's climate, location, flora, fauna and terrain affect the ability of people to provide food for consumption and for export, which ultimately has an impact on a country's economic growth. Diamond notes that all societies and cultures have had approximately similar abilities to manipulate nature, but the raw materials with which they had to start were different.

Africa's broad economic experience shows that the abundance of land and natural resources does not guarantee economic success, however. In the second half of the twentieth century, natural-resource dependence has proved to be a developmental curse, rather than a blessing. For example, many African countries were unable to capitalize on commodity windfalls of the 1970s, leaving their economies in a state of economic disaster (the good news is that at least five African countries – Chad, Equatorial Guinea, Gabon, Nigeria and Sudan – have had the good sense this time around to establish savings funds and to put aside some of their commodity windfalls). Having squandered much of their natural wealth through questionable investment and even, in some cases, outright theft, oil- and mineral-rich countries such as Nigeria, Angola, Cameroon and the Democratic Republic of Congo recorded dismal economic results in this period. They had nothing to show for it.

In 'Africa: Geography and Growth', an Oxford University and ex-World Bank economist, Paul Collier, adopts a nuanced approach to the endowments issue by classifying African countries in three groups: countries which are resource-poor but have coast-line; those that are resource-poor and landlocked; and countries which are resource-rich (where it matters little whether the country is landlocked or has a coastline). The three groups have remarkably different growth patterns. Historically, on an economic performance basis, coastal resource-scarce countries performed significantly better than their resource-rich counterparts whether landlocked or coastal; leaving the landlocked, resource-scarce economies as the worst performers. Collier reckons that these factors cost these economies around one percentage point of growth. This is a pattern which exists globally as well as being true for the African continent. Unfortunately, Collier notes, Africa's population is heavily pooled around the landlocked and resource-scarce countries.

Clearly one's environment matters, and of course the conditions in parts of Africa are harsh – notably the climate and terrain. But, harsh as they may be, these aspects are not insurmountable. With average summer temperatures reaching 49°C (120°F) Saudi Arabia is rather hot, and, of course, Switzerland is landlocked, but these factors have not stopped them from getting on with it.

Historical factors, such as colonialism, have also often been put forward as explanations for Africa's underachievement; the idea being that colonial powers delineated nations, established political structures and fashioned bureaucracies that were fundamentally incompatible with the way of life of indigenous populations. Forcing traditionally rival and warring ethnic groups to live together under the same flag would never make nation-building easy. The ill-conceived partitioning of Africa at the 1885 Berlin Conference did not help matters. The gathering of fourteen nations (including the United States, and with Germany, Britain, France and Portugal the most important participants) produced a map of Africa littered with small nations whose arbitrarily drawn borders would always make it difficult for them to stand on their own two feet – economically and politically.[1]

There is, of course, the largely unspoken and insidious view that the problem with Africa is Africans – that culturally, mentally and physically Africans are innately different. That, somehow, deeply embedded in their psyche is an inability to embrace development and improve their own lot in life without foreign guidance and help.

It is not the first time in history that cultural norms, social mores or religious beliefs have been cited as the reasons for differences in development between different peoples. The German political economist and sociologist Max Weber argued that a Protestant work ethic contributed to the speed of technological advancement and explained the development seen in industrial Britain and other European nations.

In his mind there were two broad groups: the Calvinists, who believed in predestination and, depending on their lot, may or may not acquire wealth; and the believers in the Protestant work ethic who could advance through the sweat of their brow. As with Weber, Africa's development quandary offers two routes: one in which Africans are viewed as children, unable to develop on their own or grow without being shown how or made to; and another which offers a shot at sustainable economic development – but which requires Africans be treated as adults. The trouble with the aid-dependency model is, of course, that Africa is fundamentally kept in its perpetual childlike state.

Another argument posited for Africa's economic failures is the continent's disparate tribal groupings and ethno-linguistic make-up. There are roughly 1,000 tribes across sub-Saharan Africa, most with their own distinct language and customs. Nigeria with an estimated population of 150 million people has almost 400 tribes; and Botswana with just over one million inhabitants has at least eight large tribal groupings. To put this in context, assuming Nigeria's ratio, imagine Britain with its population of 60 million divided into some 160 ethnically fragmented and distinct groupings.

At least two potential concerns face nations with strong tribal divisions. The most obvious is the risk that ethnic rivalry can lead to civil unrest and strife, sometimes culminating in full-blown civil war. In contemporary times the ghastly examples of Biafra in Nigeria (1967–70) and the ethnically motivated genocide in Rwanda in the 1990s loom large.

Paul Collier postulates that the more a country is ethnically divided, the greater the prospect of civil war. This is why, it is argued, Africa has a much higher incidence of civil war than other developing regions such as South Asia in the last thirty years. Very little can rival a civil war when it comes to ensuring a country's (and potentially its neighbours') decline – economically, socially, morally. In pure financial terms Collier has estimated that the typical civil war costs around four times annual GDP. In Africa, where small countries exist in close proximity with one another, the negative spillover cost of war onto neighbouring countries can be as much as half of their own GDP.

Even during peaceful times, ethnic heterogeneity can be seen to be an impediment to economic growth and development. According to Collier, the difficulty of reform in ethnically diverse small countries may account for why Africa persisted with poor policies for longer than other regions. Ethnically diverse societies are likely to be characterized by distrust between disparate groups, making collective action for public service provision difficult. This is particularly true in (even nominally) democratic societies, where the prospect of achieving policy consensus amongst fractious ethnically split groups can be challenging. Invariably, where there is infighting, an impasse or split across ethnic lines slows down the implementation of key policies that could spur economic growth. Kenya's turbulent democratic elections in 2008 are a recent example where tribal tensions between the presidential incumbent Mwai Kibaki (a Kikuyu) and Raila Odinga (a Luo) seeped into and infected the political process and institutions (the compromise was a coalition government made from the two groupings).

No one can deny that Africa has had its fair share of tribal fracas. But by the same token it is also true that there are a number of African countries where disparate groups have managed to coexist perfectly peacefully (Botswana, Ghana, Zambia, to name three). In the quest for a solution to Africa's economic woes, it is futile to cite ethnic differences as an excuse – born a Zulu, always a Zulu. But Zulus, like people from any other tribe, can and do intermarry; they live, work and play in integrated cities. In fact people in African cities live in a more integrated way than you might find in other cities – there are no ethnic zones such as exist in Belfast, London or New York, for that matter. Besides, once locked into the ethnic argument there is no obvious policy prescription: it's a dead end. Better to look to a world where all citizens can freely participate in a country's economic prosperity, and watch the divisive role of ethnicity evaporate.

Yet another explanation put forward for Africa's poor economic showing is the absence of strong, transparent and credible public institutions – civil service, police, judiciary, etc.

In *The Wealth and Poverty of Nations*, David Landes argues that the ideal growth and development model is one guaranteed by political institutions. Secure personal liberty, private property and contractual rights, enforced rule of law (not necessarily through democracy), an ombudsman-type of government, intolerance towards private rent-seeking and optimally sized government are mandatory.

In *Empire: How Britain Made the Modern World*, Niall Ferguson points to the common-law system and the British-type civil administration as two institutions that promoted development. Ferguson also notes that it is a country's underlying legal and political institutions that make it conducive to investment (and counter-disinvestment through less capital flight) and innovation. This necessarily includes enforcement of the rule of law, avoidance of excessive government expenditures and constraints on the executive. In turn, this yields a transparent fiscal system, an independent monetary authority and a regular securities market that foster the growth in size and number of corporations.

Professor Dani Rodrik from Harvard University is equally adamant in arguing that institutions that provide dependable property rights, manage conflict, maintain law and order, and align economic incentives with social costs and benefits are the foundation of long-term growth. In his book *In Search of Prosperity*, Rodrik points to China, Botswana and Mauritius as examples of countries which largely owe their economic success to the presence (or creation) of institutions that have generated market-oriented incentives, protected the property rights of current and future investors, and deterred social and political instability. (Botswana had a GDP per capita of US$8,170 in 2002, more than four times the sub-Saharan-Africa average, US$1,780, much of its success attributed to the probity of its political institutions.)[2]

Conversely, he suggests, Indonesia and Pakistan are countries where, in the absence of good public institutions, growth has been difficult to achieve on a sustained basis. Even when growth has occurred intermittently it has been fragile (as in post-1997 Indonesia) or incapable of delivering high levels of social outcomes in areas such as health or education (as in the case of Pakistan). Rodrik's estimates imply that changes in institutions can close as much as three quarters of the income gap between the nations with the best and those with the worst institutions.

While public institutions – the executive, the legislature and the judiciary – exist in some form or fashion in most African countries (artefacts of the colonial period), apart from the office of the president their real power is minimal, and subject to capricious change. In strong and stable economic environments political institutions are the backbone of a nation's development, but in a weak setting – one in which corruption and economic graft reign supreme – they often prove worthless.

Africa's failure to generate any meaningful or sustainable long-run growth must, ostensibly, be a confluence of factors: geographical, historical, cultural, tribal and institutional. Indeed, it would be naïve to discount outright any of the above arguments as contributing to Africa's poor growth history. However, it is also fair to say that no factor should condemn Africa to a permanent failure to grow. This is an indictment Africa does not deserve. While each of these factors may be part of the explanation in differing degrees, in different countries, for the most part African countries have one thing in common – they all depend on aid.

Does aid work?

Since the 1940s, approximately US$1 trillion of aid has been transferred from rich countries to Africa. This is nearly US$1,000 for every man, woman and child on the planet today. Does aid work? Proponents of aid point to six proofs that it can.

The Marshall Plan

First, there is the Marshall Plan. As discussed earlier, between 1948 and 1952 the United States transferred over US$13 billion (around US$100 billion in today's terms) to aid in the reconstruction of post-Second World War Europe. By most historical accounts the Marshall Plan was an overwhelming success in rebuilding the economies of war-torn Europe. The Marshall Plan not only guaranteed economic success, but many credit the programme with the re-establishment of political and social institutions crucial for

Western Europe's on-going peace and prosperity. Although the idea of aid to Africa was born out of the success of the Marshall Plan in Europe, in practical terms the two are completely different. Pointing to the Marshall Plan's achievements as a blueprint for a similar outcome for Africa tomorrow is simply wrong.

Why?

For one thing, European countries were not wholly dependent on aid. Despite the ravages of war, Western Europe's economic recovery was already underway, and its economies had other resources to call upon. At their peak, Marshall Plan flows were only 2.5 per cent of the GDP of the larger recipients like France and Germany, while never amounting to more than 3 per cent of GDP for any country for the five-year life of the programme. In marked contrast, Africa has already been flooded with aid. Presently, Africa receives development assistance worth almost 15 per cent of its GDP – or more than four times the Marshall Plan at its height. Given Africa's poor economic performance in the past fifty years, while billions of dollars of aid have poured in, it is hard to grasp how another swathe of billions will somehow turn Africa's aid experience into one of success.

The Marshall Plan was also finite. The US had a goal, countries accepted the terms, signed on the dotted line, money flowed in, and at the end of five years the money stopped. In contrast to the Marshall Plan's short, sharp injection of cash, much of Africa has received aid continually for at least fifty years. Aid has been constant and relentless, and with no time limit to work against. Without the inbuilt threat that aid might be cut, and without the sense that one day it could all be over, African governments view aid as a permanent, reliable, consistent source of income and have no reason to believe that the flows won't continue into the indefinite future. There is no incentive for long-term financial planning, no reason to seek alternatives to fund development, when all you have to do is sit back and bank the cheques.

Crucially, the context of the Marshall Plan also differed greatly from that in Africa. All the war-torn European nations had had the relevant institutions in place in the run-up to the Second World

War. They had experienced civil services, well-run businesses, and efficient legal and social institutions in place, all of which had worked. All that was needed after the war was a cash injection to get them working again. Marshall Plan aid was, therefore, a matter of reconstruction, and not economic development. However damaged, Europe had an existing framework – political, economic and physical; whereas despite the legacy of colonial infrastructure Africa was, effectively, undeveloped. Building, rather than rebuilding, political and social institutions requires much more than just cash. An influx of billions of dollars of aid, unchecked and unregulated, will actually have helped to undermine the establishment of such institutions – and sustainable longer-term growth. In a similar vein, the recent and successful experience of Ireland, which received vast sums of (mainly European) aid, is in no way evidence that aid could work in Africa. For, like post-war Europe, Ireland too had all the institutions and political infrastructure required for aid to be monitored and checked, thereby to make a meaningful economic impact.

Finally, whereas Marshall Plan aid was largely (specifically) targeted towards physical infrastructure, aid to Africa permeates virtually every aspect of the economy. In most poor countries today, aid is in the civil service, aid is in political institutions, aid is in the military, aid is in healthcare and education, aid is in infrastructure, aid is endemic. The more it infiltrates, the more it erodes, the greater the culture of aid-dependency.

The IDA graduates

Aid proponents point to the economic success of countries that have in the past relied on aid, but no longer do so. These countries are known as the International Development Association (IDA) graduates. They comprise twenty-two of some of the most economically successfully emerging countries of recent times – including, Chile, China, Colombia, South Korea, Thailand and Turkey, with only three from Africa: Botswana, Equatorial Guinea (its improvements mainly spurred by its oil find) and Swaziland.[3]

Supporters of aid suggest that these countries have meaningfully lowered poverty, increased incomes and raised their standards of living, thanks to large-scale aid-driven interventions.

However, as in the case of the Marshall Plan, their aid flows have been relatively small – in this instance, generally less than 10 per cent of national income – and their duration short. Botswana, which is often touted as a prime example of the IDA graduate success story, did receive significant foreign assistance (nearly 20 per cent of the country's national income) in the 1960s. It is true that between 1968 and 2001 Botswana's average real per capita economic growth was 6.8 per cent, one of the highest growth rates in the world. However, aid is not responsible for this achievement. Botswana vigorously pursued numerous market economy options, which were key to the country's success – trade policy left the economy open to competition, monetary policy was kept stable and the country maintained fiscal discipline. And crucially, by 2000, Botswana's aid share of national income stood at a mere 1.6 per cent, a shadow of the proportion it commands in much of Africa today. Botswana succeeded by ceasing to depend on aid.

With conditionalities

Aid supporters also believe in conditionalities. This is the notion that the imposition of rules and regulations set by donors to govern the conditions under which aid is disbursed can ultimately determine its success or failure. In the 1980s conditionalities attached to African aid policies would become the mantra.

The notion of a quid pro quo around aid was not new. Marshall Plan recipients had been required to adhere to a strict set of conditions imposed upon them by the US. They had a choice . . . you take it or you leave it. African countries faced the same choice.

Donors have tended to tie aid in three ways. First, it is often tied to procurement. Countries that take aid have to spend it on specific goods and services which originated from the donor countries, or a group selected by them. This extends to staff as well: donors employ their own citizens even when suitable candidates for the job exist in the poor country. Second, the donor can reserve the right to preselect the sector and/or project that their aid would support. Third, aid flows only as long as the recipient country agrees to a set of economic and political policies.

With stabilization and structural adjustment in vogue, the adoption of market-based policies became the requirement upon which aid would be granted. Aid would be contingent on African countries' willingness to change from statist, centrally planned economies towards market-driven policies – reducing the civil service, privatizing nationalized industries and removing trade barriers. Later democracy and governance would make their way onto the list, in the hope of limiting corruption in all its forms.

On paper, conditionalities made sense. Donors placed restrictions on the use of aid, and the recipients would adhere. In practice, however, conditionalities failed miserably. Paramount was their failure to constrain corruption and bad government.

A World Bank study found that as much as 85 per cent of aid flows were used for purposes other than that for which they were initially intended, very often diverted to unproductive, if not grotesque ventures. Even as far back as the 1940s, international donors were well aware of this diversion risk. In 1947, Paul Rosenstein-Rodin, the Deputy Director of the World Bank Economics Department, remarked that 'when the World Bank thinks it is financing an electric power station, it is really financing a brothel'.

But the point here is that conditionalities were blatantly ignored, yet aid continued to flow (and a great deal of it), even when they were openly violated. In other research, Svensson found 'no link between a country's reform effort or fulfilment of conditionality and the disbursement rate of aid funds', proving once again that though a central part of many aid agreements, conditionalities did not seem to matter much in practice.

Aid success in good policy environments

Faced with mounting evidence that aid has not worked, aid proponents have also argued that aid would work, and did work, when placed in good policy environments, i.e. countries with sound fiscal, monetary and trade policies. In other words, aid would do its best, when a country was in essentially good working order. This argument was formalized in a seminal paper published by World Bank economists Burnside and Dollar in 2000. (Quite why a country in working order would need aid, or not seek other better, more transparent forms of financing itself, remains a mystery.)

Donors soon latched onto the Burnside–Dollar result and were quick to put the findings into practice. In 2004, for example, the US government launched its US\$5 billion Millennium Challenge Corporation aid campaign motivated by the idea that 'economic development assistance can be successful only if it is linked to sound policies in developing countries'.[4] In later empirical work, the Burnside–Dollar result failed to stand up to scrutiny, and it soon lost its allure. It was not long before the wider economic community concluded that the Burnside–Dollar findings were tenuous and certainly not robust; perhaps eventually coming to the obvious conclusion that countries with good policies – like Botswana – would tend to make progress unassisted, and that a key point of aid is to help countries with bad ones. But even setting aside empirical analysis, there are, as discussed later, valid concerns that, far from making any improvement, aid could make a good policy environment bad, and a bad policy environment worse.

On the subject of good policy environments, aid supporters are convinced that aid works when it targets democracy, because only a democratic environment can jump-start economic growth. From a Western perspective, democracy promises the lot.

There are, in fact, good reasons for believing that democracy is a leading determinant of economic growth, as almost invariably the body politic bleeds into economics. Liberal democracy (and the political freedoms it bestows) protects property rights, ensures checks and balances, defends a free press and guards contracts. Political scientists such as Douglass North have long asserted democracy's essential links with a just and enforceable legal framework.

Democracy, the argument goes, gives a greater percentage of the population access to the political decision-making process, and this in turn ensures contract enforcement through an independent judiciary. Not only will democracy protect you, but it will also help you better yourself. Democracy promises that businesses, however small, will be protected under the democratic rule of law. Democracy also offers the poor and disadvantaged the opportunity to redress any unfair distribution via the state.

It is after all under democratic governments, the American economist and social scientist Mancur Olson posited, that the protection of property rights and the security of contracts, crucial for stimulating economic activity, were more likely. In essence, democracy engenders a peace dividend, introduces a form of political stability that makes it a precursor for economic growth. In Olson's world, democratic regimes engage in activities that assist private production in two ways: either by maintaining a framework (regulatory, legal, etc.) for private activity or by directly supplying inputs which are not efficiently delivered by the market (for example, a road connecting a small remote village to a larger trading town). By their very nature, democracies have an incentive to provide public goods which benefit each and everyone, and wealth creation is more likely under democratic regimes than non-democracies, such as, say, autocratic or dictatorial regimes.

Under this sky, democracy is seen as Africa's economic salvation: erasing corruption, economic cronyism, and anticompetitive and inefficient practices, and removing once and for all the ability for a sitting incumbent to capriciously seize wealth. Democracies pursue more equitable and transparent economic policies, the types of policies that are conducive to sustainable economic growth in the long run.

Moreover, the Nobel Laureate Amartya Sen argues that because democratically elected policymakers run the risk of losing political office, they are more vigilant about averting economic disasters.[5] Among mainly developing economies another study found that democratically accountable governments met the basic needs of their citizens by 'as much as 70 per cent more' than non-democratic states.[6] But, perhaps most of all, donors are convinced that across the political spectrum democracy (and only democracy) is positively correlated to economic growth.

Although the potential positive aspects of democracy have dominated discourse (and aid policy), Western donors and policymakers have essentially chosen to ignore the protests of those who argue that democracy, at the early stages of development, is irrelevant, and may even be harmful. In an aid-dependent environment such views are easy to envisage. Aid-funded democracy does not guard against a government bent on altering property rights for its own benefit. Of course, this lowers the incentive for investment and chokes off growth.

The uncomfortable truth is that far from being a prerequisite for economic growth, democracy can hamper development as democratic regimes find it difficult to push through economically beneficial legislation amid rival parties and jockeying interests. In a perfect world, what poor countries at the lowest rungs of economic development need is not a multi-party democracy, but in fact a decisive benevolent dictator to push through the reforms required to get the economy moving (unfortunately, too often countries end up with more dictator and less benevolence). The Western mindset erroneously equates a political system of multi-party democracy with high-quality institutions (for example, effective rule of law, respected property rights and an independent judiciary, etc.). But the two are not synonymous.

One only has to look to the history of Asian economies (China, Indonesia, Korea, Malaysia, Singapore, Taiwan and Thailand) to see how this is borne out. And even beyond Asia, Pinochet's Chile and Fujimori's Peru are examples of economic success in lands bereft of democracy. The reason for this 'anomaly' is that each of these dictators, whatever their faults (and there were many), was able to ensure some semblance of property rights, functioning institutions, growth-promoting economic policies (for example, in fiscal and monetary management) and an investment climate that buttressed growth – the things that democracy promises to do. This is not to say that Pinochet's Chile was a great place to live; it does, however, demonstrate that democracy is not the only route to economic triumph. (Thanks to its economic success Chile has matured into a fully fledged democratic state, with the added accolade of, in 2006, installing South America's first woman President – Michelle Bachelet.)

The obvious question to ask is, has foreign aid improved democracy in Africa? The answer to this is yes – certainly in terms of the number of African countries that hold elections, although still many of them are illiberal (people go the polls, but in some places the press remains restricted, and the rule of law fickle).

The real question to ask is, has the insertion of democracy via foreign aid economically benefited Africa? To this question the answer is not so clear. There are democratic countries in Africa that continue to struggle to post convincing growth numbers (Senegal, at just 3 per cent growth in 2006), and there are also decidedly undemocratic African countries that are seeing unprecedented economic growth (for example, Sudan).

What is clear is that democracy is not the prerequisite for economic growth that aid proponents maintain. On the contrary, it is economic growth that is a prerequisite for democracy; and the one thing economic growth does not need is aid.

In 'What Makes Democracies Endure?' Przeworski et al. offer this fascinating insight – 'a democracy can be expected to last an average of about 8.5 years in a country with a per capita income under US$1,000 per annum, 16 years in one with income between US$1,000 and US $2,000, 33 years between US$2,000 and US$4,000 and 100 years between US$4,000 and US$6,000 . . . Above US$6,000, democracies are impregnable . . . [they are] certain to survive, come hell or high water.' It *is* the economy, stupid.

No one is denying that democracy is of crucial value – it's just a matter of timing.

In the early stages of development it matters little to a starving African family whether they can vote or not. Later they may care, but first of all they need food for today, and the tomorrows to come, and that requires an economy that is growing.

Aid effectiveness: a micro–macro paradox

There's a mosquito net maker in Africa. He manufactures around 500 nets a week. He employs ten people, who (as with many African countries) each have to support upwards of fifteen relatives. However hard they work, they can't make enough nets to combat the malaria-carrying mosquito.

Enter vociferous Hollywood movie star who rallies the masses, and goads Western governments to collect and send 100,000 mosquito nets to the afflicted region, at a cost of a million dollars. The nets arrive, the nets are distributed, and a 'good' deed is done.

With the market flooded with foreign nets, however, our mosquito net maker is promptly put out of business. His ten workers can no longer support their 150 dependants (who are now forced to depend on handouts), and one mustn't forget that in a maximum of five years the majority of the imported nets will be torn, damaged and of no further use.

This is the micro–macro paradox. A short-term efficacious intervention may have few discernible, sustainable long-term benefits. Worse still, it can unintentionally undermine whatever fragile chance for sustainable development may already be in play.

Certainly when viewed in close-up, aid appears to have worked. But viewed in its entirety it is obvious that the overall situation has not improved, and is indeed worse in the long run.

In nearly all cases, short-term aid evaluations give the erroneous impression of aid's success. But short-term evaluations are scarcely relevant when trying to tackle Africa's long-term problems. Aid effectiveness should be measured against its contribution to long-term sustainable growth, and whether it moves the greatest number of people out of poverty in a sustainable way. When seen through this lens, aid is found to be wanting.

That said, the approach to food aid (launched at the 2005 Food Aid conference in Kansas City[7]) has tried to push aid in a new direction, one which can potentially help African farmers. The proposal would allow a quarter of the food aid of the United States Food For Peace budget to be used to buy food in poor countries, rather than buying only American-grown food that has to then be shipped across oceans. Instead of flooding foreign markets with American food, which puts local farmers out of business, the strategy would be to use aid money to buy food from farmers within the country, and then distribute that food to the local citizens in need. In terms of the mosquito net example, instead of giving malaria nets, donors could buy from local producers of malaria nets then sell the nets on or donate them locally. There needs to be much more of this type of thinking.

Between 1950 and the 1980s, the US is estimated to have poured the equivalent of all the combined aid given to fifty-three African countries between 1957 and 1990 into just one country, South Korea. Some have alleged that this is the kind of financial lift that Africa will need; essentially an equivalent of its own Marshall Plan.

Advocates of aid argue that aid works – it's just that richer countries have not given enough of it. They argue that with a 'big push' – a substantial increase in aid targeted at key investments – Africa can escape its persistent poverty trap; that what Africa needs is more aid, much more aid, in massive amounts. Only then will things start to truly get better.

In 2000, 189 countries signed up to the Millennium Development Goals (MDG).[8] The eight-point action plan was aimed at health, education, environmental sustainability, child mortality, and alleviating poverty and hunger. In 2005, the programme was costed. An additional aid boost of US$130 billion a year would be needed to achieve the MDG in a number of countries. Two years after the MDG pledge the United Nations held an international conference on Financing for Development in Monterrey, Mexico, where donors promised to increase their aid contributions from an average of 0.25 per cent of their GNP to 0.7 per cent, in the belief that this additional US$200 billion annually would finally address Africa's continuing problems. In practice, most of the donor pledges have gone unmet and proponents of aid have latched on to this failure to meet the pledged commitments as a reason for why Africa has been held back. But the big-push thinking brushes over one of the underlying problems of aid, that it is fungible – that monies set aside for one purpose are easily diverted towards another; not just any other purpose, but agendas that can be worthless, if not detrimental, to growth. Proponents of aid themselves have acknowledged that unconstrained aid flows always face the danger of being egregiously consumed rather than invested; of going into private pockets, instead of the public purse. When this happens, as it so often does, no real punishments or sanctions are ever imposed. So more grants mean more graft.

One of the most depressing aspects of the whole aid fiasco is that donors, policymakers, governments, academicians, economists and development specialists know, in their heart of hearts, that aid doesn't work, hasn't worked and won't work. Commenting on at least one aid donor, the Chief Economist at the British Department of Trade and Industry remarked that 'they know its crap, but it sells the T-shirts'.[9]

Study, after study, after study (many of them, the donors' own) have shown that, after many decades and many millions of dollars, aid has had no appreciable impact on development. For example, Clemens et al. (2004) concede no long-term impact of aid on growth. Hadjimichael (1995) and Reichel (1995) find a negative relationship between savings and aid. Boone (1996) concludes that aid has financed consumption rather than investment; and foreign aid was shown to increase unproductive public consumption and fail to promote investment.

Even the *most* cursory look at data suggests that as aid has increased over time, Africa's growth has decreased with an accompanying higher incidence of poverty. Over the past thirty years, the most aid-dependent countries have exhibited growth rates averaging *minus* 0.2 per cent per annum.

For most countries, a direct consequence of the aid-driven interventions has been a dramatic descent into poverty. Whereas prior to the 1970s most economic indicators had been on an upward trajectory, a decade later Zambia lay in economic ruin. Bill Easterly, a New York University professor and former World Bank economist, notes that had Zambia converted all the aid it had received since 1960 into investment, and all of that investment to growth, it would have had a per capita GDP of about US$20,000 by the early 1990s.[10] Instead, Zambia's per capita GDP was lower than in 1960, under US$500. In effect, Zambia's GDP should have been at least thirty times what it is today. And between 1970 and 1998, when aid flows to Africa were at their peak, poverty in Africa rose from 11 per cent to a staggering 66 per cent. That is roughly 600 million of Africa's billion people trapped in a quagmire of poverty – a truly shocking figure.

The evidence against aid is so strong and so compelling that even the IMF – a leading provider of aid – has warned aid supporters about placing more hope in aid as an instrument of development than it is capable of delivering. The IMF has also cautioned governments, donors and campaigners to be more modest in their claims that increased aid will solve Africa's problems. If only these acknowledgements were a catalyst for real change.

What is perhaps most amazing is that there is no other sector, whether it be business or politics, where such proven failures are allowed to persist in the face of such stark and unassailable evidence.

So there we have it: sixty years, over US$1 trillion dollars of African aid, and not much good to show for it. Were aid simply innocuous – just not doing what it claimed it would do – this book would not have been written. The problem is that aid is not benign – it's malignant. No longer part of the potential solution, it's part of the problem – in fact aid *is* the problem.

4. The Silent Killer of Growth

In 2004, the British envoy to Kenya, Sir Edward Clay, complained about rampant corruption in the country, commenting that Kenya's corrupt ministers were 'eating like gluttons' and vomiting on the shoes of the foreign donors. In February 2005 (prodded to make a public apology for his statements given the political mael-strom his earlier comments had made), he apologized – saying he was sorry for the 'moderation' of his language, for underestimating the scale of the looting and for failing to speak out earlier.[1]

If the world has one picture of African statesmen, it is one of rank corruption on a stupendous scale. There hardly seem any leaders who haven't crowned themselves in gold, seized land, handed over state businesses to relatives and friends, diverted billions to foreign bank accounts, and generally treated their countries as giant personalized cash dispensers. According to Transparency International, Mobutu is estimated to have looted Zaire to the tune of US$5 billion; roughly the same amount was stolen from Nigeria by President Sani Abacha and placed in Swiss private banks (later US$700 million of the loot was returned to Nigeria).[2] It's not, of course, just one person who has taken the money. There are many people, at many different levels of the bureaucracy, who have funnelled away billions of dollars over the years. Corruption is a way of life.

The list of corrupt practices in Africa is almost endless. But the point about corruption in Africa is not that it exists: the point is that aid is one of its greatest aides. This is not to say that there are not other facilitators of corruption. In Africa, natural-resource windfalls, such as oil, have tended to be more of a curse than a blessing. Like aid, they are susceptible to theft and have provided practically unlimited opportunities for personal wealth accumulation and self-aggrandizement.

The crucial difference between foreign aid and natural-resource endowments is, of course, that aid is an active and deliberate policy aimed at development. Countries don't have much of a choice as to whether or not they end up with an oil endowment; although of course they do have a choice on how windfalls are dealt with. With mounting pressure for greater transparency in the oil, gas and mining sectors, from organizations like the Extractive Industries Transparency Initiative (EITI),[3] the days of blatant looting and corruption in these sectors are surely numbered. But donors continue to sit in comfortable air-conditioned rooms in the West and pen the tragic fate of countries they ostensibly seek to help.

The vicious cycle of aid

With aid's help, corruption fosters corruption, nations quickly descend into a vicious cycle of aid. Foreign aid props up corrupt governments – providing them with freely usable cash. These corrupt governments interfere with the rule of law, the establishment of transparent civil institutions and the protection of civil liberties, making both domestic and foreign investment in poor countries unattractive. Greater opacity and fewer investments reduce economic growth, which leads to fewer job opportunities and increasing poverty levels. In response to growing poverty, donors give more aid, which continues the downward spiral of poverty.

This is the vicious cycle of aid. The cycle that chokes off desperately needed investment, instils a culture of dependency, and facilitates rampant and systematic corruption, all with deleterious consequences for growth. The cycle that, in fact, perpetuates underdevelopment, and guarantees economic failure in the poorest aid-dependent countries.

Corruption and growth

Ultimately, Africa's goal is long-term, sustainable economic growth, and the alleviation of poverty. This cannot occur in an environment where corruption is rife. There are, of course, any number of ways in which corruption retards growth.

In a context of high degrees of corruption and uncertainty, fewer entrepreneurs (domestic or foreign) will risk their money in business ventures where corrupt officials can lay claim to its proceeds, so investment stagnates, and falling investment kills off growth.

Development agencies would have us believe that aid helps build a lasting, credible and strong civil service. Indeed, the World Bank recommends that by providing more aid rich countries actually assist in the fight against corruption. Thanks to aid, poor governments can afford to support ethics training, increase the salaries of their public-sector employees (police, judges, medical staff, tax collectors), thereby limiting the need for corruption. Moreover, higher salaries will attract competent and higher-quality employees to the civil service.

Unfortunately, unfettered money (the prospect of sizeable ill-gotten gains) is exceptionally corrosive, and misallocates talent. In an aid-dependent environment, the talented – the better-educated and more-principled, who should be building the foundations of economic prosperity – become unprincipled and are drawn from productive work towards nefarious activities that undermine the country's growth prospects. Those who remain principled are driven away, either to the private sector or abroad, leaving the posts that remain to be filled by the relatively less-educated, and potentially more vulnerable to graft.

Endemic corruption also targets public contracts. In these environments, contracts which should be awarded to those who can deliver on the best terms, in the best time, are given to those whose principal aim is to divert as much as possible to their own pockets. What ensue are lower-quality infrastructure projects, and enfeebled public services, to the detriment of growth.

Similarly, the allocation of government spending suffers as corrupt officials are likely to choose projects less on the basis of public welfare and more on the opportunities for extorting bribes and diverting funds. The bigger the project, the greater the opportunity. Projects whose exact value is difficult to monitor present lucrative opportunities for corruption – it is easier to siphon money from large infrastructure projects than from textbooks or teachers' salaries.

So how badly does corruption actually affect growth?

Every year, since 1995, Transparency International has published a Corruption Perceptions Index (CPI). Using surveys reflecting the perceptions of business people and country analysts, the CPI ranks over 100 countries, from 0 to 10, the most corrupt to the least.

Using the Transparency International CPI, Graf Lambsdorff found that a one-point improvement in a country's corruption score was correlated with an increase in productivity of 4 per cent of GDP. This implies that were Tanzania (placed at 3.2 out of 10 on the 2007 Transparency International index) to improve its corruption score to the level of the UK (ranked 8.4 out of 10), its GDP could be more than 20 per cent higher, and net annual per capita inflows would increase by 3 per cent of GDP.

Joel Kurtzman found that every one-point increase in a country's opacity index (the degree to which a country lacks clear, accurate and easily discernible practices governing business, investment and government) correlated to a lower per capita income by US$986 and a 1 per cent decrease in net foreign direct investment as a share of GDP.[4] Moreover, corruption was also related to a 0.5 per cent increase in the country's average borrowing rate, and a 0.5 per cent increase in its rate of inflation.

Aid and corruption

The donor community is publicly airing concerns that development assistance earmarked for critical social and economic sectors is
being used directly or indirectly to fund unproductive and corrupt
expenditures (UNDP's Human Development Report, 1994). At
a hearing before the United States Senate Committee on Foreign
Relations in May 2004, experts argued that the World Bank has
participated (mostly passively) in the corruption of roughly
US$100 billion of its loan funds intended for development.[5] When
the corruption associated with loans from other multilateral-
development banks is included, the figure roughly doubles to
US$200 billion. Others estimate that of the US$525 billion that
the World Bank has lent to developing countries since 1946, at
least 25 per cent (US$130 billion) has been misused. Vast sums of
aid not only foster corruption – they breed it.

Aid supports rent-seeking – that is, the use of governmental
authority to take and make money without trade or production of
wealth. At a very basic level, an example of this is where a government official with access to aid money set aside for public welfare
takes the money for his own personal use. Obviously, there cannot
be rent-seeking without a rent. And because foreign aid (the rent)
is fungible – easily stolen, redirected or extracted – it facilitates
corruption. Were donor conditionalities remotely effective, this
would not be the case. But, as described previously, conditionalities
carry little punch.

In 'Do Corrupt Governments Receive Less Foreign Aid?',
Alesina and Weder conclude that aid tends to increase corruption.
Svensson shows how aid fosters corruption by reducing public
spending; that by increasing government revenues, aid lowers the
provision of public goods (things that everyone benefits from, but
no one wants to pay for – for instance, a lamppost). In a similar
vein, foreign aid programmes, which tend to lack accountability
and checks and balances, act as substitutes for tax revenues. The
tax receipts this releases are then diverted to unproductive and

often wasteful purposes rather than productive public expenditure (education, health infrastructure) for which they were ostensibly intended. In Uganda, for example, aid-fuelled corruption in the 1990s was thought to be so rampant that only 20 cents of every US$1 dollar of government spending on education reached the targeted local primary school.[6]

Aid goes to corrupt countries

If it is so obvious, as it must be to everyone involved, that aid is vulnerable to such blatant manipulation, why is it that donors continue to donate?

Witness the occurrences in 1978 after the IMF appointed Irwin Blumenthal to a post in the central bank of what was then Zaire, now the Democratic Republic of Congo. Blumenthal resigned in less than a year, writing a memo which said that 'the corruptive system in Zaire with all its wicked manifestations' is so serious that there is 'no (repeat no) prospect for Zaire's creditors to get their money back'. Shortly after the Blumenthal memo, the IMF gave Zaire the largest loan it had ever given to an African country and over the next ten years President Mobutu's kleptocracy had received an additional US$700 million from the Fund.

More recently, referring to Zambia's former President Chiluba (who was in power between 1991 and 2002) in a parliamentary address in 2002, Zambia's current President, Levy Mwanawasa, alleged embezzlement and theft of up to US$80 million. Yet during the period when the thefts occurred Zambia had received upwards of US$1.5 billion from the World Bank. Much of the money was given under the auspices of the Heavily Indebted Poorest Country (HIPC) debt relief programme, a programme that required its beneficiaries to be corruption-free.

More generally, the academic Larry Diamond observes that development agencies continue to give aid to the most corrupt and unaccountable African states, with known authoritarian and corrupt governments. His list includes Cameroon, Angola, Eritrea, Guinea and Mauritania, each receiving aid equalling or even exceeding the African average of US$20 per capita. There is no end to it.

Why give aid if it leads to corruption?

Given what we know about foreign aid, and how it encourages and sustains corruption, why do Western governments insist on parcelling out aid to poor countries? Beyond the motivations for aid-giving discussed earlier – economic, political and moral – there are two other practical explanations why.

First, there is simply a pressure to lend. The World Bank employs 10,000 people, the IMF over 2,500; add another 5,000 for the other UN agencies; add to that the employees of at least 25,000 registered NGOs, private charities and the army of government aid agencies: taken together around 500,000 people, the population of Swaziland. Sometimes they make loans, sometimes they give grants, but they are all in the business of aid (the total of concessional loans – those which carry a small interest rate – and grants – effectively free money), seven days a week, fifty-two weeks a year, and decade after decade.

Their livelihoods depend on aid, just as those of the officials who take it. For most developmental organizations, successful lending is measured almost entirely by the size of the donor's lending portfolio, and not by how much of the aid is actually used for its intended purpose. As a consequence, the incentives built into the development organizations perpetuate the cycle of lending to even the most corrupt countries. Donors are subject to 'fiscal year' concerns: 'they feared the consequences within their agencies of not releasing the funds in the fiscal year for which they were slated' (Ravi Kanbur). Any non-disbursed amounts increase the likelihood that their subsequent aid programmes will be slashed. With the added corollary, of course, that their own organizational standing is placed in jeopardy.

For many donor agencies the decision to lend to less than reputable governments is couched in the view that if they didn't, the poor would suffer, health and education budgets wouldn't be met, and countries would falter. The reality is, the poor aren't getting the money and, besides, even under the aid regime, African countries are faltering anyway.

Donors have the added fear that were they not to pump money in, poor countries would not be able to pay back what they already owe, and this would affect the donors' financing themselves. This circular logic is exactly what keeps the aid merry-go-round humming.

The insatiable need to lend is yet another reminder of why the conditionalities imposed on poor countries are worth no more than the paper they are written on. A 1992 study conducted by the World Bank's Operations Evaluation Department concluded that the release of aid tranches was close to 100 per cent, even when country compliance rates on conditions were below 50 per cent. Another World Bank study, in 1997, shows that between 1980 and 1996 72 per cent of the aid the World Bank allocated to adjustment lending went to countries with poor track records on compliance with conditionality. In the donor's desperate quest to lend, and maintain the lender–borrower see-saw, the aid relationship tips in favour of the corrupt government. Almost to the absurd point where the donor has a greater need for giving the aid than the recipient has for taking it.

Second, donors are apparently unable to agree on which countries are corrupt and which are not. A classic example of this occurred on 26 November 2002, when the *New York Times* published an article entitled 'Bush Plan Ties Foreign Aid to Free Market and Civic Rule'. The article trumpeted Washington's aid initiative and went on to outline the details of a White House proposal to set up a competition among the poorest world economies, where the 'winners' would be apportioned a slice of the US$5 billion foreign aid fund.

Curiously, among the list of possible qualifying countries was Malawi. Only weeks prior to the Bush announcement, Malawi's Ministry of Agriculture had been embroiled in a very public altercation with the IMF. Grain consignments had gone missing, and a sizeable percentage of Malawi's population was facing starvation. To make matters worse, a top Malawian official at the state-run grain marketing board who was to be a key witness in the two corruption cases 'mysteriously disappeared'.[7] Yet even with these allegations of corruption the US government did not see fit to remove Malawi from the qualifying Millennium Challenge Account list.

On the other hand, Tanzania was omitted from the same US Millennium Challenge Account list (apparently for reasons of corruption). But bizarrely it had been hailed as a model of good governance in November 2001 by the British government's Secretary of Development at the time, Clare Short, who promptly announced that Tanzania would benefit from a new pilot aid programme.

Who was right?

Thus, it would appear that regardless of who you are, and what you've done (or haven't for that matter), you'll get the cash from somewhere. In the Malawi maize scandal, the IMF resumed its lending programme to the government with no clear resolution of the case.

Corruption: positive or negative?

Maybe it wouldn't be so bad if African leaders, like some of their Asian counterparts, reinvested stolen money domestically, instead of squirrelling it away in foreign bank accounts.

This notion of 'positive' corruption goes a long way to explaining why many Asian countries, perceived to have high levels of corruption (in some cases, such as Indonesia, exceeding those of Africa), nevertheless post enviable levels of economic growth. For example, despite ranking just 3.5 out of 10 on Transparency International's Corruption Perceptions Index (2007), China continues to attract the greatest amount of foreign direct investment (US$78 billion in 2006, according to the IMF's International Financial Statistics), which undoubtedly has contributed to its stellar growth. Similarly, although in the 1980s Thailand registered a strong economic performance, in the same decade it was ranked the most corrupt country in the world.

In stark contrast, corruption analysts estimate at least US$10 billion – nearly half of Africa's 2003 foreign aid receipts – depart Africa every year.[8] It is this 'negative corruption' which bleeds Africa's public purse dry, and does nothing to address the continent's desperate needs. It is truly tragic that while stolen aid monies sit and earn interest in private accounts abroad, the countries for which the money was destined have stagnated, and even regressed.

The cornerstone of development is an economically responsible and accountable government. Yet, it remains clear that, by providing funds, aid agencies (inadvertently?) prop up corrupt governments. But corruption is not the only problem emanating from aid. The deleterious effects of any new aid flows would be both social and economic.

Aid and civil society

Africa needs a middle class: a middle class that has vested economic interests; a middle class in which individuals trust each other (and have a court to go to if the trust breaks down) and that respects and defends the rule of law; a middle class that has a stake in seeing its country run smoothly and under a transparent legal framework; a middle class (along with the rest of the population) that can hold its government accountable. Above all, a middle class needs a government that will let it get ahead.

This is not to imply that Africa does not have a middle class – it does. But in an aid environment, governments are less interested in fostering entrepreneurs and the development of their middle class than in furthering their own financial interests. Without a strong economic voice a middle class is powerless to take its government to task. With easy access to cash a government remains all-powerful, accountable only (and only then nominally) to its aid donors. Inhibited in its growth, the middle class never reaches that critical mass that historically has proven essential for a country's economic and political success.

In most functioning and healthy economies, the middle class pays taxes in return for government accountability. Foreign aid short-circuits this link. Because the government's financial dependence on its citizens has been reduced, it owes its people nothing.

A well-functioning civil society and politically involved citizenry are the backbone of longer-term sustainable development. The particular role of strong civil society is to ensure that the government is held accountable for its actions, through fundamental civil reforms other than simply holding elections. However, foreign aid perpetuates poverty and weakens civil society by increasing the burden of government and reducing individual freedom.

An aid-driven economy also leads to the politicization of the country – so that even when a middle class (albeit small) appears to thrive, its success or failure is wholly contingent on its political allegiance. So much so, as Bauer puts it, that aid 'diverts people's attention from productive economic activity to political life', fatally weakening the social construction of a country.

Aid and social capital: a matter of trust

Social capital, by which is meant the invisible glue of relationships that holds business, economy and political life together, is at the core of any country's development. At its most elemental level, this boils down to a matter of trust.

As discussed earlier, among development practitioners there is increasing acknowledgement that 'soft' factors – such as governance, the rule of law, institutional quality – play a critical role in achieving economic prosperity and putting countries on a strong development path. But these things are meaningless in the absence of trust. And while trust is difficult to define or measure, when it is not there the networks upon which development depends break down or never even form.

Foreign aid does not strengthen the social capital – it weakens it. By thwarting accountability mechanisms, encouraging rent-seeking behaviour, siphoning off scarce talent from the employment pool, and removing pressures to reform inefficient policies and institutions, aid guarantees that in the most aid-dependent regimes social capital remains weak and the countries themselves poor. In a world of aid, there is no need or incentive to trust your neighbour, and no need for your neighbour to trust you. Thus aid erodes the essential fabric of trust that is needed between people in any functioning society.

Aid and civil war

According to the Stockholm International Peace Research Institute, 'Africa is the most conflict ridden region of the world, and the only region in which the number of armed conflicts is on the increase.' During the 1990s there were seventeen major armed conflicts in Africa alone, compared to ten (in total) elsewhere in the world. Africa is also the region that receives the largest amount of foreign aid, receiving more per capita in official development assistance than any other region of the world.

There are three fundamental truths about conflicts today: they are mostly born out of competition for control of resources; they are predominately a feature of poorer economies; and they are increasingly internal conflicts.

Which is why foreign aid foments conflict. The prospect of seizing power and gaining access to unlimited aid wealth is irresistible. Grossman argues that the underlying purpose of rebellion is the capture of the state for financial advantage, and that aid makes such conflict more likely. In Sierra Leone, the leader of the rebel Revolutionary United Front was offered the vice-presidential position in a peace deal, but refused until the offer was changed to include his chairmanship of the board controlling diamond-mining interests. So not only would it appear that aid undermines economic growth, keeping countries in states of poverty, but it is also, in itself, an underlying cause of social unrest, and possibly even civil war.

While acknowledging that there are other reasons for conflict and war – for example, the prospect of capturing natural resources such as oil, or tribal conflict (which, of course, can have its roots in economic disparity) – in a cash-strapped/resource-poor environment the presence of aid, in whatever form, increases the size of the pie that different factions can fight over. For example, Maren blames Somalia's civil wars on competition for control of large-scale food aid.

Furthermore, in an indirect manner, by lowering average incomes and slowing down economic growth (according to Collier, both in themselves powerful predictors of civil wars), aid increases the risk of conflict.[9] In the past five decades, an estimated 40 million Africans have died in civil wars scattered across the continent; equivalent to the population of South Africa (and twice the Russian lives lost in the Second World War).

Beyond politicization of the political environment, aid fosters a military culture. Civil wars are by their very nature military escapades. Whoever wins stays in power through the allegiance of their military. Thus, the reigning incumbent, anxious to hang on to power, and manage competing interest groups and factions, first directs what resources he has into the pockets of his army, in the hope that it will remain pliant and at bay.

The economic limitations of aid

Any large influx of money into an economy, however robust, can cause problems. But with the relentless flow of unmitigated, substantial aid money, these problems are magnified; particularly in economies that are, by their very nature, poorly managed, weak and susceptible to outside influence, over which domestic policymakers have little control. With respect to aid, poor economies face four main economic challenges: reduction of domestic savings and investment in favour of greater consumption; inflation; diminishing exports; and difficulty in absorbing such large cash influxes.

Aid reduces savings and investment

As foreign aid comes in, domestic savings decline; that is, investment falls. This is not to give the impression that a whole population is awash with aid money, as it only reaches relatively few, very select hands. With all the tempting aid monies on offer, which are notoriously fungible, the few spend it on consumer goods, instead of saving the cash. As savings decline, local banks have less money to lend for domestic investment. Economic studies confirm this hypothesis, finding that increases in foreign aid *are* correlated with declining domestic savings rates.

Aid has another equally damaging crowding-out effect. Although aid is meant to encourage private investment by providing loan guarantees, subsidizing investment risks and supporting co-financing arrangements with private investors, in practice it discourages the inflow of such high-quality foreign monies. Indeed, in some empirical work, it is shown that private foreign capital and investment fall as aid rises. This may in part reflect the fact that private investors tend to be uncomfortable about sending their money to countries that are aid-dependent, a point elaborated on later in the book.

An outgrowth of the crowding-out problem is that higher aid-induced consumption leads to an environment where much more money is chasing fewer goods. This almost invariably leads to price rises – that is, higher inflation.

Aid can be inflationary

Price pressures are twofold. Aid money leads to increased demand for locally produced goods and services (that is, non-tradables such as haircuts, real estate and foodstuffs), as well as imported (traded) goods and services, such as tractors and TVs. Increased domestic demand needn't be harmful in itself, but a disruptive injection of money can be.

There are multiple knock-on effects. For example, take this very basic and simplistic story. Suppose a corrupt official gets

US$10,000. He uses some of the cash to buy a car. The car seller can now afford to buy new clothes, which places cash in the hands of the clothes trader, and so on and so forth down the line, at each point putting more pressure on domestic prices as there are now more people demanding more cars, clothes, etc. This is at least an example of positive corruption. But in a poor environment, there aren't any more cars, there aren't any more clothes, so with increased demand prices go up. Eventually, there may be more cars and there may be clothes, but by that time inflation will have eroded the economy, all the while with even more aid coming in. Perhaps ironically, because of the deteriorating inflationary environment more aid is pumped in to 'save the day'; we're back on the cycle again.

As if that was not bad enough, in order to combat the cycle of inflation, domestic policymakers raise interest rates. But, at a very basic level, higher interest rates mean less investment (it becomes too costly to borrow to invest); less investment means fewer jobs; fewer jobs mean more poverty; and more poverty means more aid.

Aid chokes off the export sector

Take Kenya. Suppose it has 100 Kenyan shillings in its economy, which are worth US$2. Suddenly, US$10,000 worth of aid comes in. No one can spend dollars in the country, because shopkeepers only take the legal tender – Kenyan shillings. In order to spend the aid dollars, those who have it must convert it to Kenyan shillings. All the while there are only still 100 shillings in the economy; thus the value of the freely floating shilling rises as people try to offload the more easily available aid dollars. To the detriment of the Kenyan economy, the now stronger Kenyan currency means that Kenyan-made goods for export are much more expensive in the international market, making the traded goods sector uncompetitive (if wages in that sector do not adjust downwards). All things being equal, this chokes off Kenya's export sector.

This phenomenon is known as Dutch disease, as its effects were first observed when natural gas revenues flooded into the Netherlands in the 1960s, devastating the Dutch export sector and increasing unemployment. Over the years economic thinking has extended beyond the specifics of this original scenario, so that any large inflow of (any) foreign currency is seen to have this potential effect.

Even in an environment where the domestic currency is not freely floating, but rather its exchange rate remains fixed, the Dutch disease phenomenon can occur. In this case, the increased availability of aid money expands domestic demand, which again can lead to inflation. Aid flows spent on domestic goods would push up the price of other resources that are in limited supply domestically – such as skilled workers – making industries (mainly the export sector) that face international competition and depend on that resource more uncompetitive, and almost inevitably they close.

The IMF has stated that developing countries that rely on foreign capital are more prone to their currencies strengthening. Accordingly, aid inflows would strengthen the local currency and hurt manufacturing exports, which in turn reduces long-run growth. IMF economists have argued that the contribution of aid flows to a country's rising exchange rate was one reason why aid has failed to improve growth, and that aid may very well have contributed to poor productivity in poor economies by depressing exports.

In other work, their research finds strong evidence consistent with aid undermining the competitiveness of the labour-intensive or exporting sectors (for example, agriculture such as coffee farms). In particular, in countries that receive more aid, export sectors grow more slowly relative to capital-intensive and non-exportable sectors.

Aid inflows have adverse effects on overall competitiveness, wages, export sector employment (usually in the form of a decline in the share of those in the manufacturing sector) and ultimately growth. Given the fact that manufacturing exports are an essential vehicle for poor countries to start growing (and achieving sustained growth), any adverse effects on exports should *prima facie* be a cause for concern.

Moreover, because the traded-goods sector can be the main source of productivity improvements and positive spillovers associated with learning by doing that filter through to the rest of the economy, the adverse impact of aid on its competitiveness retards not just the export sector, but also the growth of the entire economy.

In the most odd turn of events, the fact that aid reduces competitiveness, and thus the traded sector's ability to generate foreign-exchange earnings, makes countries even more dependent on future aid, leaving them exposed to all the adverse consequences of aid-dependency. What is more, policymakers know that private-to-private flows like remittances do not seem to create these adverse aid-induced (Dutch disease) effects, but they largely choose to ignore these private capital sources.

As a final point, in order to mitigate the Dutch disease effects (and depending on their economic environments), policymakers in poor countries generally have two choices. They can (in a fixed exchange rate regime) either raise interest rates to combat inflation to the inevitable detriment of the economy, or they can 'sterilize' the aid inflows.

Sterilization implies that the government issues bonds or IOUs to people in the economy, and in return they get the cash in the economy. Through this process the government can mop up the excess cash that aid brings in. But, as discussed later, even sterilization has its costs.

Aid causes bottlenecks: absorption capacity

Very often, poor countries cannot actually use the aid flows granted by rich governments. At early stages of development (when countries have relatively underdeveloped financial and institutional structures) there is simply not enough skilled manpower, or there are not enough sizeable investment opportunities, to put the vast aid windfalls effectively to work. Economic researchers have found that countries with low financial development do not have the absorptive capacity for foreign aid. In countries with weak financial systems, additional foreign resources do not translate into stronger growth of financially dependent industries.

What happens to this aid money that can't be used? In the most honest of outcomes, if the government did nothing with the aid inflow, the country would still have to pay interest on it. But given the policy challenges of large inflows discussed earlier (for example, inflationary pressure, Dutch disease effects), policymakers in the poor country must do something. Since they cannot put all the aid flows to good use (even if they wanted to), it is more likely than not that the aid monies will be consumed rather than invested (as before, thereby raising the risk of higher inflation).

To avert this sharp shock to the economy, African policymakers have to mop up the excess cash; but this costs Africans money. In addition to having to pay the interest on the aid the country has borrowed, the process of sterilizing the aid flows (again, issuing local–country debt in order to soak up the excess aid flows in the economy) can impose a substantial hit to the government's bottom line. Uganda offers a telling example of this. In 2005, the Ugandan central bank issued such aid-related bonds to the tune of US$700 million; the interest payments alone on this cost the Ugandan taxpayer US$110 million annually.

Naturally, the process of managing aid inflows is particularly painful when the interest costs of the debt the government pays out are greater than the interest it earns from holding all the mopped-up aid money.

Aid and aid-dependency

Corruption, inflation, the erosion of social capital, the weakening of institutions and the reduction of much-needed domestic invest-ment: with official aid to the continent at 10 per cent of public expenditure, and at least 13 per cent of GDP for the average

country, Africa's continual aid-dependency throws up a host of
other problems.

Aid engenders laziness on the part of the African policymakers.
This may in part explain why, among many African leaders, there
prevails a kind of insouciance, a lack of urgency, in remedying
Africa's critical woes. Because aid flows are viewed (rightly so) as
permanent income, policymakers have no incentive to look for
other, better ways of financing their country's longer-term development. As detailed later in this book, these options, like foreign
direct investment and accessing the debt markets, offer more-
diversified and greater prospects for sustainable development.

Relatedly, in a world of aid-dependency, poor countries' governments lose the need to pursue tax revenues. Less taxation might
sound good, but the absence of taxation leads to a breakdown in
natural checks and balances between the government and its
people. Put differently, a person who is levied will almost certainly
ensure that they are getting something for their taxes – the Boston
tea party's 'No taxation without representation'.

Besides, any rational government should be thinking about
different forms of taxation as a way of running their affairs. In
today's culture of aid-dependency, were aid to disappear (as unlikely as it seems), a country's tax-raising mechanisms would have
atrophied to a point of incapacity.

Large sums of aid, and a culture of aid-dependency, also encourage governments to support large, unwieldy and often unproductive public sectors – just another way to reward their cronies. In
his research, Boone (1996) finds that aid does increase the size of
the government.

The net result of aid-dependency is that instead of having a
functioning Africa, managed by Africans, for Africans, what is left
is one where outsiders attempt to map its destiny and call the
shots. Given the state of affairs, it is hardly surprising that, though
ostensibly high on the global agenda, the Africa discourse has been
usurped by pop stars and Western politicians. Rarely, if ever, are
the Africans elected by their own people heard from on the global
stage. And even though, as discussed earlier, the balance of power

may have shifted supposedly in favour of the African policymakers, it is still the donors who are in the policymaking driving seat (which might help explain why, over the last five decades, independent African policymaking and national economic management have diminished considerably). So aid-dependency only further undermines the ability of Africans, whatever their station, to determine their own best economic and political policies. Such is the all-pervasive culture of aid-dependency that there is little or no real debate on an exit strategy from the aid quagmire.

Aid objections

Dead Aid is not the first critique to be levelled against aid as a development tool. One of the earliest critics of aid was a Hungarian-born London School of Economics economist, Peter Bauer. At a time when the pro-aid model enjoyed wide support, Bauer was a lone dissenting voice, many of his writings drawing on his personal experience as a colonial officer studying the rubber industry in Malaysia and Nigeria. He saw what should have been flourishing industries wrecked by huge aid subsidies that rarely reached the indigent in the recipient country.

Aid, Bauer argued, interfered with development as the money always ended up in the hands of a small chosen few, making aid a 'form of taxing the poor in the west to enrich the new elites in former colonies'. Bauer argued most strongly that aid-based theories and policies were wholly inconsistent with sound economic reasoning and, indeed, with reality. Although he was a favourite of the British Prime Minister, Margaret Thatcher (she gave him a peerage[10]), at the time of his death in 1992 Peter Bauer was an outcast from the state-led socialist development agenda and his critique of the aid-based development strategy remained largely ignored.

More recently, the author and former World Bank economist Bill Easterly has provided numerous case studies on the failures of aid policies across the developing world. In *The Bottom Billion*,

Paul Collier criticizes the blanket one-size-fits-all aid approach as paying no heed to the unique circumstances of individual countries, and thus proposes a more nuanced approach to aid-driven proposals, and only where they are needed.

Perhaps where all this literature falls down somewhat is that it does not explicitly offer Africa a menu of alternatives to aid. But, more importantly, the people who actually and actively implement the aid agenda are yet to be convinced. These are the people who are so wedded to aid that they are unable to see Africa as anything but helpless without aid intervention.

What follows is a discussion of other, better ways for Africa to finance its economic development; ways that have been tried and tested in places as far-flung as India, Russia and Chile, and even, closer to home, in South Africa.

PART II

A World without Aid

The Republic of Dongo

Population: 30 million. Average life expectancy: forty years (down from sixty-five in the past twenty years, mainly because of the HIV–AIDS epidemic; in its cities, one in three adults have the disease). Annual per capita income: US$300, with 70 per cent of its population living on below US$1 a day. Average growth rate in the past twenty years was 1 per cent and 5 per cent in the last five years: has benefited from a recent copper price surge. Chief exports: copper, gold, cotton and sugar. Political system: adopted a nominal democracy ten years ago, having spent twenty years as a one-party state led by the same political party, and the same president.

This is the Republic of Dongo. While fictitious, the Republic of Dongo is not far off the reality of many African countries. Freed from European colonial rule in the 1960s, the country's background and evolution are pretty characteristic of the average African country. A socialist economy in the 1970s, it underwent privatization in the mid-1980s, moved to a democratic regime after *Glasnost* and *Perestroika*,[1] and is ranked 3 out of a possible 10 on the Transparency International Corruption Perceptions Index (where 0 is the least transparent). In the 1980s the country had accrued as much as US$3 billion of debt – twice as much as the country's annual GDP, and more than three times its combined education and health budgets. Dongo benefited from debt relief in the early part of the 2000s, which left minimal debt. Yet the country remains the beneficiary of millions of dollars of aid each year. Aid share of GDP: 10 per cent. Aid as a percentage of government revenues: 75 per cent.

Like Nigeria and Malawi, Dongo was granted its independence in the 1960s. Like Uganda and Botswana, it is struggling under the weight of HIV–AIDS. Like Zambia, Mali, Benin and the

Democratic Republic of Congo, Dongo relies on commodities (mineral and agricultural) as a primary source of export revenue (by comparison, 60 per cent of Zambia's export revenues come from copper, and over 95 per cent of Nigeria's export earnings are from oil and gas). Although not as extreme as the Gambia or Ethiopia, where 97 per cent of the government budget is attributed to foreign aid, Dongo's fiscal revenue is mainly aid-dependent. Like Kenya, it has in place a fragile democracy, which under the confluence of exogenous factors is susceptible to political destabilization. And like the majority of African (and indeed most developing) countries, its population is skewed towards the young: 50 per cent of its citizens are below the age of fifteen. Faced with few obvious prospects, Dongo, like so many of its neighbours, is intensely vulnerable: a breeding ground for disaffection, unrest and civil war.

Where will its young men and women be in twenty years' time? If a country can't produce the next generation of well-educated civil servants, politicians, economists and intellectuals, then how can it not regress? Will Dongo have changed, or will it still be locked in a cycle of disappointment and despair?

This book is not about specific development policy. It is not a book about whether one way of tackling the HIV–AIDS problem is better than another, or if one education strategy yields better results than another. It is about how to *finance* the development agenda so that, whatever the development policy, economic prosperity might be realized. Dongo will only change if its fundamental model of aid-dependency is abandoned and the *Dead Aid* proposal of this book adopted wholesale, in its entirety.

The choice of development finance is at least as important as the policies a government adopts. You can have the best development policy in the world, but without the right financial tools to implement it, the agenda is rendered impotent. Put differently, it matters little whether Dongo is capitalist or socialist in development orientation – of paramount importance is how Dongo finances its economic development. Indeed, neither a capitalist nor a socialist economic agenda can be truly achieved in the longer term without a financing strategy based on free-market tools.

Implicit in the proposals that follow are financing solutions that have their roots in the free-market system. This invites the question: is it possible for a government to raise money in a free-market way and spend it on a socialist agenda (for example, provide free education and healthcare)? The answer is yes: Sweden, Denmark and Norway are just three examples. Whatever the social, political and economic ideology a country chooses, there is a menu of financial alternatives (all better than aid) that can finance its agenda.

Can a government use free-market tools and still maintain its core socialist values? The answer is not only yes, it can, but, perhaps more importantly, it has to. And even when a government finances itself using socialist-like tools (for example, high taxes), it must still rely on some market-based financing tools in order to successfully achieve its economic goals.

5. A Radical Rethink of the Aid-Dependency Model

Governments need cash

The fact of the matter is, governments need cash. This is true regardless of political leanings – whether a socialist government, which endeavours to provide all goods and services to its citizens, or a more market-driven government, which relies on the markets to provide some public goods (that is, goods and services for which there is a broad public benefit, but for which no one person bears the cost, like, again, a lamppost).

Perhaps nowhere is the role of government more crucial – as a strategist, as a coordinator and even, to some extent, as a financier – than in poor developing countries. For at the early stages of development, the nascent private sector is simply not large enough to assume a central developmental role. Traditionally, this is where aid stepped in. But, as this book has argued, aid has not delivered any meaningful or substantial economic performance. Even if it were true that aid had contributed to economic growth, there are two compelling reasons why Africa should seek alternatives to finance its development.

The donors are growing weary. As shown earlier, over the past twenty years foreign aid to Africa has been on the decline. Whether it is because donors don't believe it works, they don't have the cash or they simply don't care, the fact remains that the donors' African aid purse is slowly shrinking.

Despite the outpourings of Live 8, one survey found that the US public's desire to reduce foreign aid outranked its fear of nuclear war. In a 1980 poll 82 per cent of respondents said foreign economic assistance should be cut.[1] This may, at least in part, explain why, when it comes down to it, most donor countries have failed to meet their pledges of 0.7 per cent of GDP made in Monterrey in 2002.

Another reason for the decline in aid flows may be that donor countries are facing their own financial pressures. It has been estimated that Bush's war on terror – being fought in Iraq, Afghanistan and Pakistan – will cost the US almost US\$3 trillion.[2] Demographic shifts are putting further strain on Western economies. Increasing numbers of retirees and fewer productive young people (owing to the ageing baby boomers and lower birth rates) means increasing health costs, lower tax revenues and less to give away. And of course it is worth remembering that the 2008 credit crisis has put immense pressure on the fiscal balances of rich (and rapidly emerging) countries; yet another stark reminder that foreign donor support is an unreliable if not dangerous palliative. For African policymakers to view aid as permanent (even with the noise made by aid proponents for it to be increased) is foolhardy.

Weaning off the addiction: no one said it would be easy

Africa is addicted to aid. For the past sixty years it has been fed aid. Like any addict it needs and depends on its regular fix, finding it hard, if not impossible, to contemplate existence in an aid-less world. In Africa, the West has found its perfect client to deal to.

This book provides a blueprint, a road map, for Africa to wean itself off aid. This goal cannot be easily achieved without the co-operation of the donors. And like the challenges someone addicted to drugs might face, the withdrawal is bound to be painful. Drug-taker, or drug-pusher, in the end someone has to have the courage to say no.

What follows is a menu of alternatives to fund economic development across poor countries. If implemented in the most efficient way, each of these solutions will help to dramatically reduce Africa's dependency on aid. The alternatives to aid are predicated on transparency, do not foster rampant corruption, and through their development provide the life-blood through which Africa's social capital and economies can grow.

The *Dead Aid* proposal envisages a gradual (but uncompromising) reduction in systematic aid over a five- to ten-year period. However worthwhile the goal to reduce and even eliminate aid is, it would not be practical or realistic to see aid immediately drop to zero. Nor, in the interim, might it be desirable.

A reasonable person could, for example, argue that aid in Africa has not worked precisely because it has not been constructed with the idea of promoting growth. The politically driven aid and tied-aid examples discussed in earlier chapters underscore the point that these types of aid flows do not promote development, and nor were they intended to in the first place. That, if executed in a moderate way, Botswana's experience with aid (detailed earlier) is exactly what we would want to see: a country that began with a high ratio of aid to GDP uses the aid wisely to provide important public goods that help support good policies and sound governance that lays the foundation for robust growth. Over time, the ratio of aid to GDP would fall as a country developed. In this way, Botswana would seem like the poster-child for what aid can do in a well-managed country.

It might very well be the case that more-modest aid programmes that are actually designed to address the critical problems faced by African countries can deliver some economic value. The *Dead Aid* proposal does allow for this perspective, by leaving room for modest amounts of aid to be part of Africa's development financing strategy. Systematic aid will be a component of the *Dead Aid* proposal, but only insofar as its presence decreases as other financing alternatives take hold. The ultimate aim is an aid-free world.

6. A Capital Solution

In September 2007, Ghana issued a US$750 million ten-year bond in the international capital markets. About a month later, the Gabonese Republic followed suit, issuing a US$1 billion ten-year bond. Could Dongo do the same?

Bonds are effectively loans or IOUs. On issuing a bond, the government promises to repay the money it borrows to the lender, plus an agreed amount of interest. However, as discussed earlier, bonds issued in the commercial marketplace are fundamentally different from aid given in loans in at least three ways: first, the interest rate charged on aid loans is below (often markedly so) the going market rate; second, aid loans tend to have much longer periods over which the borrowing country has to repay (some World Bank loans are for fifty years, whereas the longest maturities in the private markets rarely exceed thirty years); third, aid transfers tend to carry much more lenient terms in cases of default or non-payment than the relatively more punitive private bond markets.

There is a plentiful history of lesser developing countries issuing bonds – dating as far back as the 1820s. By 1860, for example, Argentina and Brazil were frequent users of the international bond markets, and since then many of the world's poorest countries have, at one time or another, issued bonds. In a report, the rating agency Standard & Poor's lists as many as thirty-five African economies as having had access to the bond markets in the 1970s and 1980s.

For many of these countries, the point of issuing these bonds to international investors was to help finance their development programmes, including infrastructure, education and healthcare. Monies raised by bonds could, however, also be used to fund governments' day-to-day (current) expenditures such as on the military, civil service and trade imbalances.

Accessing the bond markets is not that hard. Having decided
to raise money by issuing bonds rather than yet again taking aid
(this might prompt the question of why an African government
would choose to do this, but following the example set by South
Africa and Botswana, a responsible government should see merit
in this financing strategy), a country must go through a number of
reasonably straightforward stages.

First, it must acquire a rating, very often obtained from reputable
internationally recognized rating agencies. The rating might not
be great, but it is nonetheless a rating. The rating is a guide to
investors of the risk involved – the likelihood that a country will
repay its loans – and therefore determines the country's cost of
borrowing.

Second, the country must woo the potential investors – those
people willing to lend to it. Very often, a country will hire a bank
to accompany its representatives on a roadshow to help make the
case to an array of investors (institutions like pension funds and
asset managers as well as private individuals) as to why they should
lend their money to the country. It is also an opportunity to show
that it can manage its borrowings in a credible way – after all,
many of these countries were not able to keep the relatively
low-interest-rate debt of the 1970s from piling up in an unsustainable way. There are good reasons to believe that the greater
desire of many African leaders to see their countries excel should
give investors the comfort that governments will fare better with
private debt flows today than in the past.

Finally, assuming the country's representatives make a compelling case for its credibility and intention to repay, and once the
loan terms are agreed upon (the maturity or length of the bond,
the cost of the bond, the currency it will be issued in), the country
gets its cash.

The market for African countries to issue bonds exists, but
only for those countries seriously intent on transforming their
economies for the better. The good news is that for countries
considering the bond markets, investor interest in emerging countries is on the rise. Traditionally only designated emerging-markets

investors sought returns in underdeveloped markets. Over time, thanks to greater information and people being more at ease with the idea of globalization and cross-border linkages, other pools of money have turned their attention to emerging economies. This has broadened a previously narrow base to encompass an almost insatiable demand from mutual funds, pension schemes, hedge funds, insurance companies and private asset managers around the world.

Moreover, as economies have stabilized, and operate under better management, investors themselves have evolved from more short-term speculators (jumping in and out to garner short-term gains) into longer-term players happy to buy and hold developing-country assets for longer periods, and even up to maturity.

While it is true that the Asian crisis of 1997, the Russian debacle in 1998 and the Argentinian default of 2001 all led to a sudden outflow of capital from the emerging markets, these proved to be hiccups in what has been a strong and growing trend of emerging-market interest. And even in those countries where money flowed out on the back of crises, in just one decade investor money has returned.

The reasons for the rapidly growing interest in emerging economies are threefold:

For one thing, investors are always looking for the next, best opportunity. And emerging-market fundamentals make a strong case for being some of the best opportunities around. Countries that exhibit strong economic performance and are seen to be on a sound and credible footing will be rewarded. At a minimum, foreign investors will be willing to lend the country the cash. However, the beauty with bonds is that their very existence lends further credibility to the country seeking funds, thereby encouraging a broader range of high-quality private investment. More credibility equals more money, equals more credibility, equals more money and so on. As part of the macroeconomic improvements, being actively seen to be making strides away from aid, and in doing so shaking off the stigma of being an aid 'basket-case', is in itself an attractive proposition to potential investors.

Second, unsurprisingly, investors are attracted to the prospect of high returns. At the most elementary level, fund managers and commercial banks are themselves rewarded for a decent appreciation on their capital. In some cases, dedicated emerging-market fund managers (those only investing in these markets) look for net returns of at least 10 per cent per annum. By and large, thanks to their rapid growth, and the relative scarcity of investment capital, it is mainly assets in emerging markets and underdeveloped countries that can deliver these high returns.

For example, in 2006, emerging-market debt gave investors a return of around 12 per cent. The performance beat the 3 per cent return for US government bonds in the same year. Moreover, emerging-market debt has almost consistently outperformed international stocks over the past ten years. Whereas the average return for emerging-market bond funds over the past five years has been 40 per cent, US equity indices have only returned 20 per cent. In 2007, emerging-market bonds returned some 35 per cent and J. P. Morgan's EMBI+ index of such bonds performed better against American government bonds by 15 per cent. Over a longer timeframe – say an eighteen-month to two-year window – experienced portfolio managers can make significant returns, averaging 25–30 per cent per annum.

More generally, historically, choosing to invest in the bonds of relatively underdeveloped economies instead of home bonds has paid off. The evidence of ten countries suggests that investors made higher returns on bond lending to foreign countries than in safer home governments; despite the former's wars and recessions, foreign bondholders got a net return premium of 0.44 per cent per annum on all bonds outstanding at any time between 1850 and about 1970.

Third, investing in the broader class of emerging markets can enhance portfolio diversification. The notion of portfolio diversification is at the core of asset management. It pertains to the need to spread your risks and rewards across investments. In essence, you diversify a portfolio to garner the same amount of returns for a reduced amount of risk. A very basic example of the diversification concept is illustrated by two separate islands, one that produces umbrellas and another that produces sunscreen. If you were to invest only in the island that produces umbrellas, you would make a fortune when it was unseasonably wet, but you would do poorly when it was a very dry year. Conversely, were you to only invest in the island that manufactures sunscreen, you would make a killing in the year when rainfall was extremely low, but would fare poorly if it were a very wet year. However, an investment in both islands could ensure you made money regardless of the climate, thereby reducing the risk to your investment (and, of course, to your expected return).

In a similar vein, portfolio managers look to spread their risk and maximize their returns by choosing across a wide variety of options. Emerging economies (and African investments as well) offer a way for portfolio managers to improve their performance.

Like the sunscreen and umbrella islands, emerging markets and developed markets are so disparate that the opportunity to enhance a portfolio's performance by having some exposure to both markets is considerable; smoothing out the risks and enhancing the returns.

In the past, research has found that emerging-market debt (broadly as a group, as well as for individual countries) has low (and sometimes even negative) correlations with other major asset classes. To put it simply, emerging-market investments tend to fare well when other asset classes (say, developed-market stocks and bonds) fare less well. Indeed, the correlation of key emerging-market spreads (the difference between the risk-free rate and the rate charged to a riskier concern) and US bond returns is typically negative – moving in the same direction when the global economy is universally bad.

Emerging-market debt has the advantage of being counter-cyclical to the developed business cycle, since, in a global recession, poor countries can find it cheaper to repay their debts. As global interest rates decline, which often occurs on the back of a global economic slowdown, the debt service costs for poor countries (denominated in the foreign currency) goes down.

Differences in economic fundamentals between developed and

developing countries also provide support for the diversification argument. Emerging-market debt also benefits from high oil prices. Although oil price shocks may induce a global economic recession (recent oil price heights have so far defied this assumption), the counter-cyclicality of emerging-market debt – the fact that oil-producing countries may fare well when oil prices rise – means emerging-market assets can help protect a more diversified portfolio.

There is an additional factor that can drive demand for the bonds of well-run African countries. Very often, international investors have restrictions on what they can and cannot buy for their portfolios. For example, some pension funds are only allowed to buy securities (stocks or bonds) which are included in approved lists (indices) drawn up by rating agencies or investment banks (for example, the J. P. Morgan Emerging Market Bond Index). Like in football or other sports, these indices are in effect league tables in which countries can go up or down, be included or excluded depending on their overall performance and their liquidity (that is, how easy it is to buy and sell the security). There is, therefore, always constant movement (South Africa, South Korea, Mexico and Brazil each have moved to higher levels of the credit league tables), and, more importantly, there is always room for new entries.

Likewise, sometimes countries leave willingly, and sometimes they are forced out.

As countries mature they may choose to reduce the number of bonds they issue in the international market in favour of domestic bond issues or relying on domestic savings and tax. South Africa is one such example. Over time, as its issuance of international bonds declined, its position in the J. P. Morgan EMBI league table fell, and eventually it was dropped. In another case, when Argentina defaulted on US\$132 billion of its debt in 2001, it was also removed from J. P. Morgan's index.

Not every investor uses league tables. For those interested in taking great risks the league tables may not matter. However, for more risk-averse investors league tables matter a lot. The point is, league table or no, there is a huge untapped market available for those African countries that choose to put themselves forward. Clearly the fluidity in these league tables is an obvious opportunity for African countries to raise their game and get on them.

Furthermore, by graduating onto such a bond index, greater name recognition and investor familiarity could improve liquidity and over time reduce a country's cost of borrowing from the international markets; another perk for being responsible and growing up. Today the total amount of hard-currency emerging-market government debt is approximately US$100 billion, and as much as US$3 trillion market trading per day.

But there are challenges. History and experience have taught us that.

As mentioned earlier, in order for borrowers (countries or companies) to access bond investors, they need a credit rating. That is the first hurdle that needs to be jumped; their credit rating determines which investors a borrower gets to see and the cost of borrowing. For the most part, there are three recognized major rating agencies that investors look to: Standard & Poor's, Moody's Investors Service and Fitch Ratings. Their role is to assess a potential borrower's ability (mainly the country's likely future income path based on economic and social factors) and willingness (essentially a political assessment) to repay any debt. On this basis countries are ranked from triple A to triple C – essentially bankrupt.

But rating countries and companies is an art not a science, and rating agencies have been known to get it wrong – sometimes spectacularly, as in the case of Enron, which had received a clean bill of health (rated a solid investment grade Baa3 by Moody's) just five days before the company filed for bankruptcy. In May 2008, the rating agency Moody's was reeling from revelations that the company had allegedly awarded incorrect ratings to securities worth at least US$4 billion because of a bug in its computer models. Although this debacle centred on rating agencies' role in rating complex (derivative) structures, rather than traditional models used to rate sovereigns and large corporates, it is clear that no one is infallible.

If a country is awarded a better credit rating than it deserves, it has little to complain about. But the reverse can happen, and this would be felt in the interest rate that the country would face upon borrowing.

A country's ratings are not only important for its own ability to issue debt, but also dictate the rating for companies within its borders. The notion of a sovereign ceiling means that a company can never obtain a credit rating higher than that of its country. In places where a country has no rating the ability for companies to seek outside investment capital is hampered greatly.

Another challenge is contagion. This is the misguided idea that all emerging countries are tarred with the same brush, and that if one defaults then inevitably all others in the same category, regardless of their unique situations, will follow suit.

The 1997 East Asian crisis is an illustration of this. Although the financial problems were initially confined to the East Asian economies, countries such as Brazil, where the stock market fell by 24 per cent, and South Africa, where it fell by 23 per cent (both in dollar terms) over the same period, also felt the pain. The Mexican tequila crisis of 1994 and the Russian flu of 1998 are other examples of how the international markets' negative reactions to one country spill over and unfairly penalize other countries.

In theory, the risk for an African government is that it could be susceptible to its neighbours' bad news and, without notice, investors could take their money out, leaving a country cash-strapped. With the bond markets effectively shut, a country's carefully scripted economic plans can be suddenly placed in jeopardy, through no fault of its own. During the East Asian crisis the average cost of borrowing for an emerging market rose by as much as 60 per cent.

The good news is that international investors no longer view the markets in such a uniform way. As investors have become savvier, the notion of contagion risk has largely diminished. When Argentina defaulted in 2001, the repercussions elsewhere were insignificant. Borrowing costs money, and some forms more than others. This is a challenge African governments must face up to.

For most poor countries, the obvious financial choice is to go for the cheapest option – that is, aid – but because of the fine print this often proves to be a costly choice. The realities of borrowing are much more nuanced. While it will always be *financially* cheaper for them to borrow from the World Bank and other concessionary lenders, factoring in other costs suggests a more punitive deal.

It all adds up. The status quo of aid-dependency guarantees reputational damage. Ever-present corruption and the negative stigma left in the minds of potential investors (another African begging bowl) are part of the hidden costs when countries access 'cheaper financing'. How much better if a country pays the higher financial rate, and gets quality investment and an improved standing in the world?

The average cost for an African government to draw down on a World Bank loan under its concessional window is around 0.75 per cent. The average cost for an emerging-market country to issue debt in 2007 was 10 per cent, but has been declining.

In just ten years, emerging-market spreads – that is, the premium developing countries have to pay in addition to the borrowing cost of a risk-free borrower (say, the United States government) – shrank from 30 per cent to a record low of 5 per cent in 2006. The narrower spread means a country issuing debt now saves an average of about US$90 million a year in interest for every US$1 billion compared to debt issued in 2002.

Why have the costs of borrowing come down? Two reasons: first, notable improvements in different countries' macroeconomic and political environments. Second, improved liquidity (save perhaps the mid-2008 credit crunch); that is, more cash chasing developing-country assets. The net result is that developing countries' assets become more attractive, and the increase in demand helps lower costs. Some emerging economies have improved so much, and have risen up the credit league tables so dramatically, that they have shed the tag of emerging markets (which bears relatively higher borrowing costs) and joined the ranks of the highest-rated countries. With this, of course, comes access to the cheapest rates of borrowing. Poland and Hungary are two examples. By 2006, because both countries had made marked improvements on the economic and political fronts, they were able to issue debt of unprecedented size (both topping the €1 billion mark) at very low borrowing cost; Hungary received the cheapest-ever pricing for a central European convergence sovereign.

Globally, developing countries are moving up credit tables. For example, the highest-quality (investment grade) share of the league table has increased from 3 to 42 per cent. And the proportion of countries remaining in the lower ranks has declined from 25 to 6 per cent. Sadly, apart from South Africa, Africa has played no part in this.

Rebounding from a default

Sometimes, factors are beyond a government's control, and these can have far-reaching ramifications for the finances of even the most stable of countries. Environmental disaster (such as the 1975 frost in Brazil which devastated its coffee crop) may force a country to default on its debt obligations.

Spain defaulted on its external debt thirteen times between 1500 and 1900. Since 1824 Venezuela has defaulted nine times. Brazil defaulted on its international debt in 1826, 1898, 1902, 1914, 1931, 1937 and 1983. Argentina defaulted in 1828, 1890, 1982, 1989 and most recently 2001.

There are costs to defaulting, not least of which is that a country drops off the credit rating league table, and its cost of borrowing skyrockets. But, though unfortunate, defaulting is not the end of the world. The debt markets are very forgiving, and investor memory is short.

As long as the borrower is seen to address its troubles, sometimes unforeseen, sometimes of its own making (governments have been known to be time-inconsistent – saying one thing today and doing another tomorrow – the 'read my lips' scenario), it can return to the market. But you can only return to the market once investors are convinced that you are politically and/or economically back on track (unfortunately, of course, aid will be given to you anyway).

The markets have rewarded reformers. For example, just three years after it defaulted on its internal debt in 1998, the international debt markets welcomed new bond issues from Russia – the City of Moscow issued a €400 million bond in November 2001.

And on the back of the Asia crisis, even though many Asian economies saw their ratings plummet and their costs of borrowing shoot up – to the point where they were effectively locked out of the capital markets until they reformed – they too were rewarded. Before the crisis, South Korea was assigned a high investment grade rating of A+ by the international rating agency Standard & Poor's. At the height of the Asia crises in 1997, it had been downgraded nine notches to a sub-investment grade B+ rating. (It went from A+ to B+ in just two months). However, by addressing investors' specific concerns on the need for the country to restructure its domestic banks, the country was upgraded to investment grade again in a year.

But Africa's defaulters have not done the same, turning away from meaningful reform, and choosing instead the deceptively easier route of aid. The typical recovery period after an emerging-market crisis has been one to two years. However, barring the Ghana and Gabon bond issues of 2007, the last time an African nation tapped the international debt markets was in the mid-1990s (Congo-Brazzaville in 1994 with a US$600 million ten-year bond issue). Of the 35-odd African countries that had issued bonds in the international capital markets around that time, virtually all of them defaulted; and in the subsequent thirty years, none of them have returned.

They have a choice of course, but African countries have not come to the markets largely because they have not wanted to. The good news is that there are signs that this is changing. A report titled 'Financial Institutions' Debt Issuance is Likely to Increase in Sub-Saharan Africa', published on 30 April 2008 on Ratings Direct, Standard & Poor's, commented on the prospects for increasing bond issuance from Africa. The international credit rating agency noted that banks from Ghana, Kenya, and the regional monetary unions of the West African Economic and Monetary Union and the Economic and Monetary Community of Central Africa would be the most likely candidates in the next two to three years to raise long-term debt.[1]

The overall trend is clearly an encouraging one. Although there is still a way to go in rating governments and corporates across Africa, over the past eighteen months Standard & Poor's has assigned long-term credit ratings to four banks in Nigeria, two of which subsequently issued debt in the international capital markets.

It is these strides that Africa desperately needs to take. The prospect of new financial players from Africa's banking and other private sectors bodes well for greater transparency and financial maturity, which will allow them to gain better access to both domestic and international capital markets. But, most of all, acquiring credit ratings and experience in the capital markets is the passport for Africa's participation in the broader world architecture.

It is incumbent on African governments to play ball. The success of the private venture into the capital markets (be they domestic or international) crucially hinges on African governments understanding the very positive economic implications of their constructive actions and grasping the opportunities the capital markets offer (better reputation, transparency, greater investment capital, longer-term reduction in borrowing costs). It also requires efficient management, and an understanding that if they are not supportive, the negative ramifications are damaging and far-reaching.

For sure, there is an institutional imperative − it is always in the interest of international banks to lend and investors to invest − but seduced by the siren call of aid, African governments sink their ships on the rocks of development demise. The discussion thus far has focused on the international debt markets, but African countries should develop their domestic bond markets as well.

The domestic bond markets are a prerequisite for a country's stock market, and yet another means for the nation's corporate sector to finance its own growth. Besides, issuing debt in the domestic markets is often cheaper than issuing debt in a foreign currency (this might explain the evolving trend in more-developed emerging countries, who have seen a shift from predominantly international debt to now roughly 70 per cent of debt in local currency). In order to pay interest and the principal on foreign debt a country has to find the foreign currency first. The risk posed by fluctuations in currencies means a borrower may have to find more of its own currency to meet the value of its foreign debt.

There have been a number of developments towards the furtherance of these domestic markets. Take the European Investment Bank (EIB), a European financing institution established in 1958 to finance capital projects which further the European Union's objectives (investing in small and medium-sized enterprises and in environmental-sustainability projects, for example).

On 11 February 2008 the EIB launched its first Zambian bond denominated in the local currency. The bond transaction was for 125 billion Zambian kwacha (US$33 million) of two-year notes. Although this was not the first time the EIB had accessed the local markets in an African country – it had already done so in local currencies in Botswana, Ghana, Mauritius, Namibia and, of course, South Africa (where it has issued local-currency denominated debt for more than ten years) – it was the first time an international entity issued debt in Zambia's local currency.

From the EIB's perspective, issuing debt in Zambia's local currency just makes good business sense. It complements the EIB's activities in Zambia as a lender in the mining industry and to small and medium-sized enterprises. Furthermore, the EIB's currency-lending activities are aligned with their funding, which makes for good currency management.

For Zambia, the EIB's transaction marked the first sale of debt in an African currency to international investors, and as with the other African countries who have executed debt transactions in local currencies, the bond issue was just another way of developing and further solidifying the country's credentials in the capital markets. It certainly helped draw the attention of international investors to the Zambian bond market. Thanks to the EIB transaction, Zambia joined a group of countries that met the criteria for issuance to the European institutional market.

The wider debt capital markets viewed the EIB transaction as an innovative way to tap funding possibilities in relevant local currencies, the clear benefit being that the bond issue was supporting the development of local currency markets as well as taking a step towards potential future lending in local currency.

The G8 took the decision to make local bond market development a core focus of its policy agenda. In response to this, and recognizing the importance of a private-sector role in finance in emerging economies, there has been movement in donor quarters.

In October 2007, the World Bank (partly at the instigation of emerging-country governments) launched its Global Emerging Markets Local Currency Bond (GEMLOC) Program, designed to 'support development of local currency bond markets and increase their investability so that more institutional investment from local and global investors can flow into local currency bond markets in developing countries'. In conjunction with private-sector participants, this is the World Bank's first concerted foray into developing the local debt markets across emerging economies.[2]

The establishment and development of local bond markets has obvious benefits to the poorest economies. Stronger, more liquid local currency bond markets can lower the cost of borrowing and reduce financing and investment mismatches and the risks they create. They support development and enhance a country's resilience to shocks, thereby improving its financial stability.

Yet, thus far, the development of the local debt capital markets in many of the poorest countries has been impeded by the absence of longer-term domestic bonds that are liquid (that is, can be easily bought or sold), and by a relatively weak regulatory and financial infrastructure.

Additionally, the level at which international investors are able/ willing to own locally denominated debt has been dismal; foreign institutional investors (such as pension funds and insurance companies) hold only around 10 per cent of their emerging-markets debt investments in local currency; this despite the arguments for holding local-currency denominated debt being so compelling. A portfolio which includes local emerging-market bonds offers diversification since correlations with other securities (stocks and bonds) are low, and potential returns from an improving credit environment and currency appreciation in emerging economies are attractive.

The GEMLOC Program has three separate but complementary parts. An investment manager would be assigned to promote investment in the local-currency bonds of emerging-market countries, as well as develop investment strategies for local-currency bond markets. Shortly after the GEMLOC announcement, the bond investment organization PIMCO was selected to fulfil the role of investment manager. Next, Markit, a private-sector data and index firm, was chosen to develop a new independent and transparent bond index, for the emerging-markets local-currency debt asset class. A country's inclusion in the new index (known as GEMX) is based on a country's score on investability indicators, such as market size, and a set of criteria developed by the ratings, risk and research firm CRISIL. The index will open the way for a broad range of countries to be considered for investment, as currently less than 2 per cent of local-currency debt is benchmarked against leading market indices, and these include relatively few countries and instruments. The GEMX index offers an opportunity for investment strategies that include a diversified set of local emerging-market bonds with low correlations and potential returns from an improving credit environment and currency appreciation.

Finally, the World Bank will provide advisory services to low- and middle-income countries to promote reforms aimed at developing local bond markets, improving their investability for domestic and international institutions, and enhancing financial stability. Many local markets have severe impediments on investability, such as red tape, taxes, weak infrastructure and inefficient debt management, all of which make investment in local markets unattractive.

The idea of this leg of the GEMLOC initiative is to improve market infrastructure and regulation, and help transform emerging local-currency bond markets into a better-known and mainstream asset class, ultimately supporting the expansion of corporate bond markets, infrastructure, and mortgage- and asset-backed financing. The hope is for involvement of the World Bank Group to cease after ten years; almost unwittingly recognizing there are other, better, private ways for emerging economies to finance their development.

Based on the current investability criteria, only two African countries are likely to be included in the bond index – Nigeria and South Africa. Because the GEMX index will focus on countries that have local sovereign bond markets of at least US$3 billion, and sovereign bond issues of at least US$100 million (as well as at least a 50 per cent minimum score on a rank of investibility), initially it is likely that the index will only include fixed-rate government sovereign bonds from twenty countries: Brazil, Chile, China, Colombia, Egypt, Hungary, India, Indonesia, Malaysia, Mexico, Morocco, Nigeria, Peru, Philippines, Poland, Russia, Slovakia, South Africa, Thailand and Turkey.

Over time, additional countries, and additional bond types (for example, company bonds), will be considered for inclusion in order to further improve liquidity. Although the stringent criteria bar many African countries from participation today, there is no reason why other African bonds should not be included over time, as their local debt markets develop. That noted, however, the high bond issuance thresholds laid out in the criteria point again to the fact that smaller African countries ought to consider more unified and integrated regional approaches to the capital markets, rather than necessarily going it alone.

Can Dongo tap the markets?

The capital markets are open, and open for Africa. Any assertions that these countries cannot tap the international capital markets are simply wrong. Developed countries tap the market, developing nations tap the market, even the World Bank taps the market (in a rather circular reasoning, to raise funds which they then lend on to African countries). Africa should tap the markets too. By and large, the countries that have not thus far issued bonds have not done so because they do not wish to, not because they can't.

The amount of emerging-market bond issuance jumped 52 per cent from US$152 billion in 2004 to US$230 billion in 2007. Currently, the total amount of bonds from government and companies in these countries stands at approximately US$1.5 trillion, of which a relatively minuscule US$10 million is from Africa. In the past ten years forty-three developing countries have issued international bonds – only three were African: South Africa, Ghana and Gabon.

However, there are early indications that more are on the way. Since 2003, fifteen African countries have obtained credit ratings (Benin, Botswana, Burkina Faso, Cameroon, Gabon, Ghana, Kenya, Lesotho, Mali, Mauritius, Mozambique, Namibia, Nigeria, Senegal and Uganda), all of which have ratings high enough to tap the bond market. In July 2006, for instance, Zambia, Africa's largest copper producer, announced it would seek its first credit ratings to enable it to sell bonds in international markets. The Governor of the country's Central Bank argued that a rating would help cut Zambia's funding costs.

The first-order problem is whether you can tap the markets, and the second is for how much. Every year governments set up their budgets in order to determine the amount of money they will need to finance their development objectives. With this figure in mind, and assuming they appreciate the many benefits bond issuance can bring, they must embark on a roadshow. From this beauty parade – their roadshows are of course competing with other countries' roadshows for a finite (albeit large) pool of cash – they can easily gauge how much investor appetite there is.

As Ghana and Gabon have both demonstrated, it is perfectly possible to raise large sums. More generally, judging by the amounts realized by countries with similar ratings, the precedence has been good. For example, Turkey, rated single BB− (similar to Gabon), and Brazil, rated BBB− (as is Namibia), have raised upwards of US$1 billion in a single bond issuance. In 2006, the average bond issue by an emerging market was US$1.5 billion.

As with everything, more experience yields greater rewards. As governments become more experienced and investors get to know a country better, countries can come to the markets more often (many emerging economies tap the markets every year) and in transactions of greater size.

Some African countries might initially be viewed as too small, or too risky, to lend to. For these (Togo, Benin and Mali, for instance), and others perceived as too hazardous for individual investments, there are three risk mitigants to consider.

One is the pooling of risk. Rather than individual countries reaching for the bond markets independently, African countries could form groups or regional coalitions, issue debt as a single entity, and divide the proceeds (and debt service obligations) accordingly. Every country would get the upside benefit of cash from the bond issue but bear the downside risk of one or many of the countries in the pool defaulting (in which case the non-defaulting countries have to repay the borrowings on behalf of the offending country or countries).

A collective bond would undoubtedly require a unified rating (which would probably be some average of all the countries participating), but, as with the umbrella and sunscreen island example before, there are notable diversification benefits to be gained. For instance, for some countries the pooled cost of borrowing would most likely be lower than that for an individual country alone – a weighted probability of default would be lower than for an individual country's bond issue. And much like the European Union (or any union of countries, for that matter) 'higher-quality' countries would be given the incentive to participate in such a structure to garner positive externalities from the neighbours' growth as well.

Pooling risk invariably introduces a free-rider problem; that is, the risk that one or more countries take relatively more cash out of the pot than they deserve (or add more risk to the pot than is desirable – although in this case the group of countries could simply choose to exclude the country, thereby forcing it to the markets on its own, to earn its stripes). A way around this problem would be to divide the spoils on a GDP-weighted basis – the bigger the country, the greater the share of the bond pie it receives; or on a needs basis (based on countries' per capita income) – the greater a country's needs, the more of the bond proceeds it would receive.

There is another risk mitigant, which is to offer some type of insurance or payment protection in the event that a country defaults. Like any other credit guarantee, the guarantor (usually of higher credit standing than the country issuing the bond) would promise to cover some part or the full value of the bond if a country reneged on the repayment of its debt obligation.

A recent example of this is South Africa's Pan-African Infrastructure Development Fund (PAIDF). Launched in 2007, the PAIDF invests in infrastructure projects (transport, energy, water and sanitation, and telecommunications) across Africa, while the South African government guarantees the fund's multi-billion-dollar investments.[3] With its respectable triple B credit rating, South Africa is effectively underwriting the risk of the whole continent, and is able to provide comfort to investors, who might otherwise see the fund's investment pool as too risky. As of October 2007, the PAIDF had raised approximately US$625 million from Africa itself (suggesting, as discussed later, that a lot of untapped cash exists on the continent).

Another innovative example in risk mitigation is that of the Republic of Argentina, which issued a US$1.5 billion bond consisting of six bonds, guaranteed in part by the World Bank. Each bond was for US$250 million maturing at different times (one year, eighteen months, two, three, four and five years).

The guarantee structure worked quite simply: the first bond was fully guaranteed by the World Bank. Once Argentina repaid this bond, the guarantee rolled forward to the second bond. Thereafter, it rolled to each successive bond, and so on.

The idea of the guarantee was that if Argentina failed to repay any bond at maturity, the World Bank would immediately step in and repay it. If Argentina then repaid the World Bank within sixty days of the bond's maturity, the guarantee of the World Bank would roll to the next bond. However, if Argentina failed to repay the World Bank within sixty days (which unfortunately it eventually did), the guarantee would be lost on all the remaining bonds. Because of the World Bank's guarantee, each of Argentina's bonds in the series achieved a highly coveted investment grade rating based on the AAA-rated guarantee of the World Bank. Despite Argentina's default on this structure, this is exactly the type of innovative financing structure that can help bring Africa into the global fold.

Finally, securitizing a bond issue can also mitigate risk and reduce the cost of borrowing. The process of securitization involves ring-fencing, or setting aside, specific cashflows to pay off a debt obligation. Take an oil-producing nation as an example of how this works. The country issues debt with the understanding that all payments (interest and principal) due on the bond will be repaid by specified income earned from oil exports. Of course, there is the risk that something happens to the income stream (again, think of the Brazilian frost and the income lost on the coffee crop), but in general investors are reassured if they can see exactly how they will be repaid their investment money.

In 'Ending Africa's Poverty Trap', the economist Jeffrey Sachs et al. estimated the money needed to meet the Millennium Development Goals (MDG) (excluding government and household contributions) for Ghana, Tanzania and Uganda. They argued that this is the amount that donors would have to provide in order to finance the MDG intervention package.

For Ghana, he estimated the total investment needs for meeting the MDG would average US$2 billion a year (or US$82.8 per year, per person). Of this total, Sachs proposed that US$1.2 billion would need to be funded by annual external assistance. Yet, although Ghana's 2007 foray in the bond markets was only for US$750 million, it was heavily oversubscribed to the tune of US$5 billion of unmet investor demand. On the basis of Sachs's estimate, this would have been enough to cover at least the foreseeable next five years' MDG requirements.

The Ghanaians did the right thing. There was clearly no need to go down the aid path yet again, and there was a lot of upside to issuing the bond. Although small this time round relative to the investor demand, their approach was prudent – and for this they will be rewarded. In particular, their initial success can be the launch-pad for them to win favour from investors and return to the market regularly in future years.

Tanzania and Uganda's MDG financial needs are far less modest (US$2.5 billion and US$1.6 billion per year, respectively) but no less unachievable. Although they are both in a position to issue bonds (Uganda has a B credit rating from the Fitch rating agency) towards meeting their MDG needs, they have yet to take the plunge.

Depressingly, and maintaining the status quo, the Sachs estimates all require a doubling of aid for each country.

7. The Chinese are Our Friends

In the summer of 2005, Lukas Lundin, an intrepid mining entrepreneur, rode his 1200cc BMW motorcycle the full length of Africa – from Cairo to Cape Town (three times the distance of New York to California). The journey would take him five weeks and cover 12,000 kilometres (roughly 8,000 miles), through ten African countries. His expedition took him past the pyramids of Egypt, through the dusty and arid terrain of Ethiopia and Sudan; through the scenic savannahs of Kenya, and past Mount Kilimanjaro in Tanzania. He rode past Lake Malawi, past the Victoria Falls in Zambia, past the Okavango swamps of Botswana, and through the Namib Desert of Namibia; concluding the treacherous ride in South Africa.

At the time, 85 per cent of the roads he travelled on were tarred – of the highest quality, no different from the ones he rode on in California. He was astonished – this was not what he had expected at all. Along the roads, in country after country, there were clues as to how this had come about: signposts proclaiming 'this road constructed with the grateful assistance of the Government of the People's Republic of China'.

As this story illustrates, there has recently been a surge of foreign direct investment aimed at Africa. It's been a long time coming, but in terms of what capital is available it barely scratches the surface.

Some figures to think about: in 2006, global flows of foreign direct investment (FDI – defined by the United Nations Conference on Trade and Development as 'an investment made to acquire a lasting interest in an enterprise operating outside the economy of the investor') soared to a record US$1.4 trillion. FDI into developing countries (globally) approached almost US$400 billion. During this period, FDI flows to the whole of sub-Saharan Africa reached a meagre US$17 billion. The continent as a whole continues to disappoint and has failed to capitalize on the phenomenon of global FDI growth. In 2006, the US$37 billion that Africa received as official foreign aid was more than twice the continent's foreign direct investment, and today Africa attracts less than 1 per cent of global capital flows, down from almost 5 per cent a decade ago.

The disappointment is justifiable. In theory, foreign capital should flow from richer countries to poor. The marginal product of a unit of capital should be higher in poor countries than in rich (in a rich country US$1 can produce only one pair of shoes, whereas in a poor country US$1 can produce ten pairs – more bang for your buck). Typically in these countries labour is more abundant and cheaper, thus increasing its appeal to FDI.[1] Japanese car markets have invested in Eastern Europe, where labour costs are low. So too have low production costs in the textile industry attracted Asian and Chinese investors to Africa – seeking both low overheads and the opportunity to use the African countries' export quota.

Yet Africa, which should on this basis be the prime target for FDI, continues to be broadly ignored. More figures: in 2006, FDI of US$200 billion accrued to only ten emerging economies (in descending order, China, Russia, Turkey, Mexico, Brazil, India, Romania, Egypt, Thailand and Chile – none in the top ten are in sub-Saharan Africa); 52 per cent of FDI went to Asia; FDI to China alone was roughly US$80 billion – five times the amount for the African continent as a whole.

So why, then, given Africa's level of development, is it that most of the capital flows have by-passed the most needy of continents?

Why FDI does not flow to Africa

Few would dispute the fact that Africa is, a priori, ready-made for FDI. Its labour costs are low, its investable opportunities are high, and even theoretically, as home to some of the poorest countries in the world, Africa should be FDI's natural suitor.

Truth be told, there are hurdles for investors to overcome. For the most part infrastructure (roads, telecommunications, power supply, etc.) is scant, and of poor quality, making the costs of overall production of goods and services (when transport costs are figured in) steep – which explains why it is cheaper to make almost anything in Asia and ship it to Europe, than produce it in Africa, although the continent is much closer.

However, physical constraints are nothing when compared with man-made disincentives: widespread corruption, a maze of bureaucracy, a highly circumscribed regulatory and legal environment, and ensuing needless streams of red-tape.

Doing business in Africa is a nightmare. The World Bank's annual 'Doing Business' survey provides data on the relative ease (or difficulty for that matter) with which business can be conducted around the world. The results are all too revealing, and do much to explain why Africa remains at the bottom of any FDI investors' list.[2]

In Cameroon, it takes an investor who seeks a business licence on average 426 days (that is almost a year and three months) to perform fifteen procedures; whereas in China it takes 336 days and thirty-seven procedures, and in the USA, only forty days and nineteen procedures. What entrepreneur starting a business in Angola wants to spend 119 days filling out forms to complete twelve procedures? He is likely to find South Korea a much more attractive business culture, as it will take him only seventeen days to complete ten procedures.

It's not only the red-tape. It's also the opacity. Investors don't know where to go, or who to ask. In a number of mining-dependent countries, rather than the government offering parcels of land in open auction, prospective investors are expected to provide the government with specific land coordinates. The geological survey offices know where the ore lies, but they just can't be bothered to help the investors along. Though the countries' livelihoods depend significantly on such entrepreneurs coming in, given the nature of doing business it is hardly surprising that this much-needed investment stays away.

It may all sound insurmountable, but just like a click of a switch it is perfectly possible (and easy) for an enterprising government to reduce the paperwork, supply the coordinates, and speed up the process. Unfortunately, the reality may not be as simple as that, but it is has been shown that improving regulations for business could lift GDP by 2.3 per cent a year (Djankov, McLiesh and Romalho). The Commission for Africa notes that Uganda's economy grew by around 7 per cent between 1993 and 2002 when the country improved its regulatory climate. It also reduced the number of people living on less than a dollar a day from 56 per cent in 1998 to 32 per cent in 2002 after the government introduced measures to attract investors.

Africa continues to have a bad reputation. The former UN Secretary-General, Kofi Annan, put it this way: 'For many people in other parts of the world, the mention of Africa evokes images of civil unrest, war, poverty, disease and mounting social problems.[3] Unfortunately, these images are not just fiction. They reflect the dire reality in some African countries, though certainly not all.'

Unless Africa does something about it, this image is bound to remain fixed in the minds of investors. Continent-wide economic growth won't accelerate unless African governments improve conditions for investment. African policymakers would do well to remember that there are other developing regions where it is much easier to generate similarly attractive returns with considerably less hassle. This is probably not accidental – their leadership just happens to care more.

What does Dongo need to do to attract FDI?

As a first port of call, Dongo needs to recognize that FDI is an engine for economic growth. Besides the welcome cash raised to support development initiatives, there are other benefits that FDI will bring: it will create more jobs, assist in the transfer of new technology, help stimulate the formation of Dongo's capital markets, improve management expertise, and aid indigenous firms

to open up to the international markets. Furthermore, satisfied
FDI investors would be happy to introduce the country to other
forms of capital – bank lending and venture capital.

The more foreign cash Dongo can attract, the more foreign cash
Dongo will get.

But Dongo has some work to do. It needs to give its moribund
legal and regulatory system teeth. Investors need to know and
believe they have some means of recourse – somewhere to go if
and when their contracts falter.

Dongo also needs to recognize that it must woo FDI investors,
who are used to being courted by all manner of other emerging
nations. Attractive tax structures are a great way of luring investors
in. For example, in order to bring in foreign mining investment
in the late 1990s, the Zambian government reduced royalties to a
minuscule 0.6 per cent. (Although on the back of the surge in
copper prices the tax rate was raised to 3 per cent.) Beyond this,
because FDI investors perceive their capital differently from bank
capital – the former looking to invest in a country over longer
periods of time than the latter – they will look to countries that are
keen, and that are seen, to invest in their infrastructure (economic,
political and social – notably education).

Although spasmodic, Africa's FDI news is not universally bad.
The UN Conference on Trade and Development (UNCTAD)
has reported that 'from the viewpoint of foreign companies, investment in Africa seems to be highly profitable, more than in most
other regions.' Japanese companies said in 1995 that they made
more profit from their African investments than from those in
South-East Asia, the Pacific, North America and Europe.[4] American investors have said that they made a return on their African
investments of 25 per cent in 1997. This is two thirds more than
they made from their investments in Asia and the Pacific, and
50 per cent more than their return on capital invested in Latin
America and the Caribbean. UNCTAD reports that British direct
investment in Africa, excluding Nigeria, increased by 60 per cent
between 1989 and 1995.

The Chinese are our friends

In the last sixty years, no country has made as big an impact on the political, economic and social fabric of Africa as China has since the turn of the millennium. It's not the first time China has been there. One of the lasting monuments to its former presence is the 1,860-km (1,160-mile) railway, built in the 1970s for US$500 million, that connects Zambia, through Tanzania, to the Indian Ocean.

More recently, China (both public and private) has launched an aggressive investment assault across the continent. China is growing at a phenomenal rate. Its economy has grown as much as 10 per cent a year over the past ten years, and it desperately needs the resources that Africa can provide. The US Energy Information Administration calculates that China accounted for 40 per cent of the total growth in oil demand over the past four years. In 2003 it overtook Japan to be the world's second-biggest consumer of petroleum products after the US.

But rather than conquer Africa through the barrel of a gun, it is using the muscle of money. According to its own statistics, China invested US$900 million in Africa in 2004, out of the US$15 billion the continent received, up from US$20 million in 1975. Roads in Ethiopia, pipelines in Sudan, railways in Nigeria, power in Ghana — these are just a few of the torrent of billion-dollar projects that China has flooded Africa with in the last five years, each one part of a well-orchestrated plan for China to be the dominant foreign force in twenty-first-century Africa.

The evidence is overwhelming. In November 2006, more than forty African leaders gathered at the first Sino-African summit — the Forum on China–Africa Cooperation – in Beijing.[5] Very nearly every African leader was there: the big, the small, the credible and the not so credible. Amidst the fanfare (the Chinese had imported giraffes and elephants as part of the revelry to make the African delegates feel more at home, and lined the streets with fifty African flags), the Chinese government unveiled its African strategy.

In his opening ceremony address, the Chinese President, Hu Jintao, told his audience: 'In all these years, China has firmly supported Africa in winning liberation and pursuing development . . . China has trained technical personnel and other professionals in various fields for Africa. It has built the Tanzam Railway and other infrastructure projects and sent medical teams and peace-keepers to Africa.'

The Chinese President went on: 'Our meeting today will go down in history, we, the leaders of China and African countries, in a common pursuit of friendship, peace, cooperation and development, are gathered in Beijing today to renew friendship, discuss ways of growing China–Africa relations and promote unity and cooperation among developing countries.' With this, he launched China's new multi-pronged assault on Africa, which would focus on trade, agricultural cooperation, debt relief, improved cultural ties, healthcare, training and, yes, even some aid (but thankfully only a small component of their strategy).

In an effort to help fast-track Africa's development, China has in recent years pledged to train 15,000 African professionals, build thirty hospitals and 100 rural schools, and increase the number of Chinese government scholarships to African students from the current 2,000 per year to 4,000 per year by 2009. In 2000, China wrote off US$1.2 billion in African debt. In 2003 it forgave another US$750 million. In 2002, China gave US$1.8 billion in development aid to African countries. In 2006 alone, China signed trade deals worth almost US$60 billion.[6]

The Chinese are moving in, and they are moving in in a big way. As well as many visits to numerous African countries by the Chinese leadership (including by the Chinese Premier, Wen Jibao), Chinese entrepreneurs, technical experts, medical staff and simply prospectors looking for that pot of gold are found everywhere.

An excerpt from an article in the *Economist* magazine in 2006 illustrates the point wonderfully well:

In his office in Lusaka, Xu Jianxue sits between a portrait of Mao Zedong and a Chinese calendar. His civil-engineering and construction business has been doing well and, with the help of his four brothers, he has also invested in a coal mine. He is bullish about doing business in Zambia: 'It is a virgin territory,' he says, with few products made locally and little competition. He is now thinking of expanding into Angola and Congo next door. When he came in 1991, only 300 Chinese lived in Zambia. Now he guesses there are 3,000.[7]

One of the most impressive aspects of the whole Chinese package to Africa is its commitment to FDI. This is achieved both directly through the government and, indirectly, by encouraging private Chinese enterprises to invest in Africa, usually through preferential loans and buyer credits.

Between 2000 and 2005, Chinese FDI to Africa totalled US$30 billion. As of mid-2007, the stock of China's FDI to Africa was US$100 billion.

China has invested billions in copper and cobalt, in the Democratic Republic of Congo and Zambia; in iron ore and platinum in South Africa; in timber in Gabon, Cameroon and Congo-Brazzaville. It has also acquired mines in Zambia, textile factories in Lesotho, railways in Uganda, timber in the Central African Republic and retail developments across nearly every capital city. However, oil is the gusher.

Almost consistently over the last decade, Nigeria and Sudan have been the largest beneficiaries of FDI in Africa. In 2004, they received more than half of Africa's FDI – Nigeria over US$4 billion and Sudan almost US$2 billion, while the rest of Africa got around US$4 billion. China's part of this has been extensive. In January 2006, the state-owned Chinese energy company, CNOOC, paid almost US$3 billion for a 45 per cent interest in a Nigerian oilfield. China has built a 900-mile pipeline and invested at least US$20 billion in Sudan.

Angola has now overtaken Saudi Arabia as China's biggest single provider of oil. In the first half of 2006, Angola alone supplied almost 20 per cent of oil imports to China, and, in total, African countries provided roughly 30 per cent of China's crude oil imports. China has shown similar interest in other producers such as

Sudan, Equatorial Guinea, Gabon and Congo-Brazzaville, which already sells almost half of its total crude exports to Chinese refiners. In 2006, 64 per cent of Sudan's oil exports went to China.

While it is true that China's African investments have, for the most part, been directed towards resource-rich countries, and thus the mining sectors, over time a much broader investment approach is becoming evident. In the last few years, for example, Chinese FDI to Africa has diversified into sectors such as textiles, agro-processing, power generation, road construction, tourism and telecommunications. Furthermore, the Chinese government has pledged to step up China–Africa cooperation in transportation, communications, water conservancy, electricity and other infrastructure. Among other transport contracts, Chinese companies are rehabilitating the legendary Benguela railway, from the coast to the borders of Zambia and the Democratic Republic of Congo, originally completed by the British in the 1920s. And in Nigeria, an US$8.3 billion deal was recently reached with a Chinese contractor to rebuild the dilapidated colonial-era railway between Lagos and the northern Nigerian city of Kano, as the first stage of a twenty-year rail modernization plan. Financial services and banking have also been in China's sights. In a move that confirmed the depth of its commitment, the Chinese state-owned Industrial and Commercial Bank bought a 20 per cent stake in Standard Bank (for US$5.5 billion), Africa's largest indigenous bank in 2007.

The list of China's involvement in Africa is endless. All but five African countries now have relations with Beijing: Burkina Faso, The Gambia, Malawi, São Tomé and Principe, and Swaziland had not yet signed up to the China–Africa Cooperation Forum at the time of writing. China's African role is wider, more sophisticated and more businesslike than any other country's at any time in the post-war period.

Objections to China in Africa

China's African charm offensive has not gone unnoticed. Criticisms abound, notably from those who currently rule the roost in determining Africa's destiny – the Western liberal consensus, who believe (often in the most paternalist way) it is their responsibility to look after Africa. But what exactly is their motivation? Is it that they care? Or is it the underlying political fear that, left unchecked, China will use Africa as a stepping stone on its relentless march towards world aggrandizement. Given the state of play, perhaps they have reason to be worried.

Whatever the case, the clamour of objections surrounding the Chinese presence in Africa grows ever louder, on a number of fronts: China's record on governance and human rights, and the suggestion that Africans (as a whole) are getting a raw deal.

The European Investment Bank (EIB) has expressed concern that the world's development banks may have to water down the social and environmental conditions they attach to loans in Africa and elsewhere because they are being undercut by Chinese lenders. In 2006, Philippe Maystadt, the EIB's President, referring to Chinese lenders said, 'they don't bother for social or human rights conditions'. Maystadt claimed Chinese banks snatched projects from under the EIB's nose in Asia and Africa, after offering to undercut the conditions it imposed on labour standards and environmental protection.

In a similar attack, in February 2007, the editor-in-chief of *Foreign Policy* magazine, Moisés Naím, expressed concern about how Chinese economic pragmatism appeared to override principles of openness pursued by Western donors. He tells of how the Chinese trumped a World Bank deal for aid to Nigeria. The country's railway system had been brought close to disuse as a result of bad management; after extensive negotiations, the World Bank and Nigerian government agreed on a US$5 million project that would allow private companies to help clean up the mess. On the point of signature, however, the Chinese stepped in with an offer of US$9 billion to rebuild the entire rail network. Nine billion dollars, no strings attached, and thus no reform required.

The fiasco of the 2008 Olympic torch multi-city stopover (London, Paris, Buenos Aires, New Delhi, St Petersburg, San Francisco and Dar-es-Salaam, to name a few) en route to Beijing serves as a reminder that China's human rights record is less than stellar, and in Africa most pointedly in Sudan. China's insatiable appetite for oil has led it into partnership with a country where in the region of Darfur more than 200,000 people have been killed.

Eyebrows were also raised when in 2005 on an African tour Premier Hu Jintao visited Zimbabwe's Robert Mugabe. (Ignoring the fact, of course, that both the US and UK have maintained diplomatic ties with Zimbabwe throughout Mugabe's regime, and as recently as 2006 international donors have given Mugabe a combined aid package of US$300 million.)

More generally, many Africans scoff at the notion that Westerners should be outraged by Chinese implicit support for Africa's corrupt and rogue leaders. It is, after all, under the auspices of Western aid, goodwill and transparency that Africa's most notorious plunderers and despots have risen and thrived – Zaire's President Mobutu, Uganda's President Idi Amin and the Central African Republic's 'Emperor' Bokassa (who kept his victims' heads in a fridge), to name just three.

African leaders appear less willing to be micro-managed than they once were – even if it is in exchange for cash. Perhaps fed up with acres of paperwork and the revolving door of commanding Western donors, or simply desperate to try out a new development model that might actually work, they are increasingly drawn to the more hassle-free, no-questions-asked China route. For Angola, for example, which has been keen to get going with the reconstruction of its infrastructure, China's straightforward approach is an attractive alternative to what is seen as the endless nit-picking of the IMF and the Paris Club of creditors, which have been quibbling over terms for years. José Cerqueira, an Angolan economist, notes that China is welcome because it eschews what he sees as the IMF's ideological and condescending attitude – 'For them, we should have ears, but no mouth.'[8]

No one can deny that China is at least in Africa for the oil, the gold, the copper and whatever else lies in the ground. But to say that the average African is not benefiting at all is a falsehood, and the critics know it.

Revealingly, despite some of the negative headlines about China's emergence in Africa, in surveying some ten African countries (Ethiopia, Ivory Coast, Ghana, Kenya, Mali, Nigeria, Senegal, South Africa, Tanzania and Uganda), the June 2007 Pew Report (entitled *Global Unease with Major World Powers*), finds that the balance of opinion regarding China is decidedly positive, reflecting, to a large extent, the widespread view that 'China's growing economic power has a positive effect on respondents' own countries, especially in the developing world'. More specifically, four important points emerge from the surveys on how many Africans view the Chinese.

First, across the continent, favourable views of China (and its investments in Africa) outnumber critical judgements by at least two to one in almost every country. In Ivory Coast and Mali more than nine in ten have a favourable view of China, and positive opinions dominate negative ones in Senegal and Kenya, where 81 per cent view China in a good light. Three quarters of those surveyed in Ghana and Nigeria hold an approving view, as do two thirds of Ethiopians. In Uganda, twice as many have a favourable view of China as unfavourable (45 per cent to 23 per cent, respectively). In terms of trends, in just the past year, favourable attitudes towards China in Nigeria rose 16 percentage points from 59 per cent to 75 per cent.

Second, in nearly all African countries surveyed, more people view China's influence positively than make the same assessment of US influence. Majorities in most African countries believe that China 'exerts at least a fair amount of influence on their countries'. In Ivory Coast, Mali and Senegal significantly more notice China's influence than America's (79, 83 and 72 per cent for China, versus 65, 66 and 54 per cent for the US, respectively).

Third, across Africa, China's influence is seen as growing faster than America's, and China is almost universally viewed as 'having a more beneficial impact on African countries than does the United States'. For example, although the vast majority of Ethiopians see both China and America having an effect on the way things are going in their country, China's influence is viewed as much more positive than America's. By a 61 to 33 per cent margin Ethiopians see China's influence as benefiting the country; whereas America's influence is viewed as more harmful than helpful, with a 54 to 34 per cent margin, respectively. The margins are even more pronounced in Tanzania, where 78 to 13 per cent believe Chinese influence to be a good thing, while 36 per cent view America's influence as a good thing versus 52 per cent a bad.

Even where countries view both Chinese and American influence as beneficial, China's involvement in Africa is viewed in a much more positive light than that of the US. For example, 86 per cent in Senegal say China's role in their country helps make things better, compared to America's 56 per cent. A similar pattern is noted in Kenya, where 91 per cent believe China's influence on their economy is good, versus America's 74 per cent.

A final point worth highlighting is that, across much of Africa, China's influence is already as noticeable as America's, and is increasing at a much more perceptible pace than America's. In Senegal, 79 per cent see China's influence as growing, as opposed to America's 51 per cent. Survey results are similar in Ethiopia, Ivory Coast and Mali.[9]

Indeed, not only are the benefits of China's African presence acknowledged, but they are also being spread more widely. Traditionally China was narrowly focused on resource interests, benefiting only a few. However, as discussed earlier, in recent years China broadened its investment horizons (now encompassing other sectors) and people are benefiting from the trickle-down effect of its resource investments – employment, housing and better standards of living. For many Africans the benefits are all too real – there are now roads where there were no roads, and jobs where there were no jobs. Instead of staring at the destructive desert of aid they can, at last, see the fruits of China's involvement, the latter clearly a factor in Africa's posting a 5 per cent growth rate in recent years.

This is not to say that Chinese FDI does not have challenges. Some are worried that Chinese companies are underbidding local firms and not hiring Africans. There are also concerns at lax safety standards around hazardous jobs – mainly in the mining and mining-related industries. This may well be the case, but this is where African governments should step in and regulate – African governments (accountable to their own people), mind you, not everyone else.

For example, in order to increase the participation of indigenous Africans in many of the industrial and mining opportunities, some African governments are legislating for a required minimum level of participation by the local population. In much the same way that South Africa introduced its Black Economic Empowerment regulations, and the US has its affirmative-action policies, Zambia recently announced the Citizens Economic Empowerment Commission, which covers similar ground.[10]

They've got what we want, and we've got what they need

Bartering infrastructure for energy reserves is well understood by the Chinese and Africans alike. It's a trade-off, and there are no illusions as to who does what, to whom and why. There are those who see China as merely using Africa for its own political and economic ends. To continue to grow at its extraordinarily rapid rate China needs fuel, and Africa has it. But for Africa it's about survival. In the immediate term, Africa is getting what it needs – quality capital that actually funds investment, jobs for its people and that elusive growth. These are the things that aid promised, but has consistently failed to deliver.

Of all the developing countries, China stands as the largest foreign investor in Africa. But it is not the only one: India, Russia, Japan, Turkey and the broader Middle East are not far behind.

In April 2008, in New Dehli, India launched its own Africa manifesto – the India–Africa Forum – promising, like China, credit lines and duty-free access to Africa.[11] Specifically, India would double its credit lines to Africa from US$2.15 billion in 2003/2004 to US$5.4 billion in 2008/2009. Not to be left out, Russian companies have also joined the gold rush. Recently, the Russian gas giant Gazprom offered to invest up to US$2.5 billion to develop Nigeria's natural-gas reserves, and in May 2008 Japan hosted the Fourth Tokyo International Conference on African Development, where forty-five African leaders and ministers were wooed, with much the same elixir – trade, aid, debt relief and infrastructure.[12]

Also in May 2008, Turkey signed mutual trade agreements with thirty-five African countries (including Burkina Faso, Cameroon, Ethiopia, Ghana, Kenya, Liberia, Nigeria, Senegal, South Africa and Tanzania), offering to trade under tax incentives and with government support.[13] More generally, the World Bank's President, Robert Zoellick, has urged Sovereign Wealth Funds (whose assets are estimated to be at least US$3 trillion) to invest 1 per cent of their proceeds in equity investment in Africa. Many of them have already done so. The pattern is clear.

From whatever perspective, it's a win–win proposition.

For Africa's investors they have money to put to work (China's reserves topped US$1 trillion in 2007), and they have economic growth they need to sustain. For Africa, besides the physical infrastructure, the growth and the jobs, there is the promise of poverty reduction, the prospect of a burgeoning middle class, scope for increased know-how and technology transfer, and ultimately more FDI.

For Dongo, the FDI opportunity knocks.

Conclusion

Despite the opportunity, current forecasts of FDI to Africa remain disappointingly low. According to the *Economist* (EIU), global FDI inflows are projected to grow at an annual average rate of

8 per cent between 2006 and 2010, whereas for Africa the share will remain at around a depressing 1.4 per cent.[14] Without sizeable and sustained investment, African workers remain unable to earn competitive wages as there is insufficient capital to invest in machinery, buildings and hardware that could make them more productive. This directly hampers Africa's prospects for growth.

The experience of countries as far-flung as Singapore, Mauritius, China and Costa Rica suggests that where there is a positive environment, FDI will flow and contribute to sustained growth. But who would want to invest their money in aid-ridden states where it is easy for others to take property away, either at gunpoint or through corruption?

Just as throwing aid money at poor countries does not work, simply boosting investment is not the key to economic growth either. Only when capital is allocated to its most productive uses will an economy benefit, and this can only happen when governments are given incentives to respect and support those industries that can contribute to a country's longer-term potential. The ceremony to cut the red ribbon to launch the newest road, bridge or port is easy. The hard part is ensuring the longevity of infrastructure, which can only be achieved if the economy is growing (tolls on toll roads only make sense if people can pay them, and they can only do so if the economy is on the move).

Because not all African countries are equal – some have fewer natural resources than others, or fewer investment opportunities – the amounts for FDI will vary from border to border. For these countries, less favoured by nature, there is yet another route to finance development that they should pursue.

8. Let's Trade

In December 2005, at the Second Conference of Chinese and African Entrepreneurs, China's Premier, Wen Jibao, pledged that China's trade with Africa would rise to US$100 billion a year within five years. Forget the capital markets, forget FDI, forget the US$40 billion a year aid programme, and forget trade with any other country in the world – this is just trade with China. Assuming that nothing else changed, that could be US$100 billion in 2010, US$100 billion in 2011, and the year after that, and the year after that, and the year after that.

By 2015, just five years later, that would be US$500 billion of trade income – 50 per cent of the trillion dollars of aid that has made its way to Africa in the past sixty years. The difference is, of course, one is laced with bromide, the other steroids.

Economic theory tells us that trade contributes to growth in at least two ways: by exactly increasing the amount of actual goods and services that a country sells abroad, and by driving up productivity of the workforce – our mosquito net maker from Chapter 3, selling 500 nets a week, could perhaps sell 1,000 were he able to export some of them abroad. To do so, his productivity would have to increase, which is good for growth.

The economic benefits of trade are, for the most part, a generally accepted truth (see Dollar; Sachs and Warner; Edwards). However, not all countries that have embraced trade have seen a concomitant rise in their growth. Indeed, countries can be classified into three broad categories: winning globalizers, who have increased trade and seen increased growth; non-globalizers, who eschew trade and have, unsurprisingly, seen little accompanying growth; and, paradoxically, the losing globalizers, who have increased trade but seen no associated growth. Tragically, many African countries fall into this third group. Why?

It all comes down to politics. In an uncertain world, Western countries (notably France and the US) are fearful of relying on other nations for their food in the event of a global war. Moreover, elected Western politicians have remained keen to protect their agricultural markets, and win the backing of the powerful farming lobby. The net result is a protective world of trade restrictions and barriers thrown up around the West, to keep African (and other developing regions') produce out. But developed markets are crucial, in terms of both purchasing power and size, for African trade, which depends on such countries for much of its export revenue.

The members of the Organization of Economic Cooperation and Development (OECD) – a club of rich nations – spend almost US\$300 billion on agricultural subsidies (based on 2005 estimates). This is almost three times the total aid from OECD countries to all developing nations (of course, some aid advocates suggest compensating Africa for this imbalance with more aid). Estimates suggest that Africa loses around US\$500 billion each year because of restrictive trade embargoes – largely in the form of subsidies by Western governments to Western farmers.

In the United States alone, the total annual amount of farm subsidies stands at around US\$15 billion, and that number is rising. As a share of farmers' income, subsidies rose from around 14 per cent in the middle of the 1990s to around 17 per cent today. The 2002 US Farm Security and Rural Investment Act gave US farmers nearly US\$200 billion in subsidies for the subsequent ten years – US\$70 billion more than previous programmes, and represented as much as an 80 per cent increase in certain subsidies.

The Europeans are just as protective. The Common Agricultural Policy (CAP) eats into around half the European Union's budget of €127 billion (direct farm subsidies alone are worth nearly €40 billion), and EU subsidies are approximately 35 per cent of farmers' total income. What this means is that each European Union cow gets US\$2.50 a day in subsidies,[1] more than what a billion people, many of them Africans, each have to live on every day.

For the West, it would appear that everything is sacred: steel, cotton, sugar, rice, wheat, corn, soybeans, honey, wool, dairy produce, peanuts, chickpeas, lentils and even mohair. These subsidies have a dual impact. Western farmers get to sell their produce to a captive consumer at home above world market prices, and they can also afford to dump their excess production at lower prices abroad, thus undercutting the struggling African farmer, upon whose meagre livelihood the export income crucially depends. With the millions of tons of subsidized exports flooding the market so cheaply, African farmers cannot possibly compete.

Look at what has happened to two of Africa's chief exports: cotton and sugar, both of which have to contend with their Western counterpart producers.

In 2003, US cotton subsidies to its farmers were around US$4 billion. Oxfam has observed: 'America's cotton farmers receive more in subsidies than the entire GDP of Burkina Faso, three times more in subsidies than the entire US aid budget for Africa's 500 million people.'

Yet, the livelihoods of at least 10 million people in West and Central Africa alone depend on revenues from cotton, including some 6 million rural households in Nigeria, Benin, Togo, Mali and Zimbabwe.

In May 2003, trade ministers from Benin, Burkina Faso, Chad and Mali filed an official complaint against the US and the EU for violating WTO rules on cotton trade, claiming that their countries together lost some US$1 billion a year as a result of cotton subsidies.

In Mali, more than 3 million people – a third of its population – depend on cotton not just to live but to survive; in Benin and Burkina Faso, cotton forms almost half of the merchandise exports. Yet thanks to subsidies, Mali loses nearly 2 per cent of GDP and 8 per cent of export earnings; Benin loses almost 2 per cent of its GDP and 9 per cent of export earnings; and Burkina Faso loses 1 per cent of GDP and 12 per cent of export earnings. Moreover, a 40 per cent reduction in the world price (that is, equivalent to the price decline that took place from December 2000 to May 2002) could imply a 7 per cent reduction in rural income in a typical cotton-producing country in West Africa like Benin.

The case of sugar is a similarly sour tale.

The US sugar industry receives US$1.3 billion of support per year, European Union producers receive US$2.7 billion, and in the two years between 1999 and 2001 the OECD supported its sugar farmers to the tune of US$6.4 billion, an amount more than the total value of sugar exports from developing countries, and 55 per cent of the US$11.6 billion annual world sugar trade.

Like cotton, sugar subsidies hurt Africa. The charity Oxfam estimated the regime has deprived Ethiopia, Mozambique and Malawi of potential export earnings of US$238 million since 2001. The costs of Mozambique's sugar losses equalled one third of its development aid from the EU and its government's spending on agriculture and rural development. The EU also supports its producers by blocking the entry of developing-country imports into its markets with tariffs of more than 300 per cent. Oxfam estimated that Malawi could have significantly increased exports to the Union in 2004 but that market restrictions deprived it of a potential US$32 million in foreign-exchange earnings, equivalent to around half the country's public-healthcare budget.

It's not just developed countries that are guilty of distorting trade markets. China is reported to support its cotton sector by an estimated US$1.5 billion annually. Turkey, Brazil, Mexico, Egypt and India put US$0.6 billion into their cotton sectors during 2001/2002.

But perhaps the most egregious examples come from Africa itself. African countries impose an average tariff of 34 per cent on agricultural products from other African nations, and 21 per cent on their own products. As a result, trade between African countries accounts for only 10 per cent of their total exports. By contrast, 40 per cent of North American trade is with other North American countries, and 63 per cent of trade by countries in Western Europe is with other Western European countries.

The glaring trade inequity has led to a lot of talk, but despite round after round of the World Trade Organization negotiations – Uruguay, 1994, Doha 2001 and on-going, et al. – all the chatter has amounted to little for Africa.

Perhaps the most notable Western efforts to level the trade

playing field have been the US African Growth and Opportunity
Act (AGOA)[2,3] of 2000, and Europe's Everything But Arms
(EBA)[4] of 2001, neither of which can claim to have made an
overwhelming impact on the state of play. This may, to some
extent, explain why Africa's share of global trade remains at around
1 per cent (having fallen from a high of 3 per cent sixty years ago),
even though Africa is commodity-rich. It seems truly bizarre that
such a large continent in population terms is pretty much irrelevant
in trade terms.

AGOA opens US markets to a range of African products,
especially textiles, on the basis that freer trade will create jobs
and reduce poverty in many sub-Saharan Africa countries. For
example, the average duty for garment imports into the US stands
at 17.5 per cent, but apparel imports from the twenty-five eligible
African countries into the US are duty-free. These imports are,
however, capped at a limit of 3 per cent of total US apparel
imports.

In 2003, AGOA exports were worth more than US$14 billion
(£7.4 billion). While the headlines look strong, the devil, again, is
in the detail. Only a handful of African countries have benefited –
and even then, most of them are the oil-rich and larger economies.
Nigeria, South Africa, Gabon and Lesotho account for more than
90 per cent of AGOA duty-free benefits, and of the total US$14
billion export value, petroleum products accounted for 80 per
cent, with textiles and clothes accounting for US$1.2 billion.

The picture is not much rosier with the EBA. The EBA is
designed to give duty- and quota-free access for the forty-eight
countries (thirty-three African nations) described by the United
Nations as 'least-developed'. But in 2001, trade in goods given
preference for the first time under its auspices amounted to just
0.02 per cent of exports by least-developed countries to the European Union. The narrow range of goods eligible, coupled with
the amounts, dramatically minimize these schemes' effectiveness.
The process can be arbitrary and absurd. For instance, whereas
T-shirts produced in war-torn Somalia are welcomed under the
EBA, shirts made in the equally deserving Kenya are excluded.[5]

As things stand in 2008, the European Union is still Africa's largest trading partner (26 per cent), followed by the United States (18 per cent), and then China at 11 per cent (Asia excluding China is 11 per cent as well). It is clear that however good their hand may seem, when trading with the West the cards are stacked against Africa, and will always be. Western political imperatives against freer trade continue to reign, and efforts to depose the current regime are proving futile. If the West wants to be moralistic about Africa's lack of development, trade is the issue it ought to address, not aid. Of course, such are the West's demands that even if all its trade barriers were lifted, Africa no longer has the technological equipment and know-how to compete on many products where it once had a comparative advantage. Together with environmental and labour issues, these are now serious barriers to trade.

Although Europe remains Africa's main trading partner, its share of the region's foreign trade has dropped to 26 per cent from 40 per cent in the ten years from 1996. It's time that Africa faced up to this fact and moved on; time that Africa sat down at another table, with another set of players – ones who deal a fairer deck. For now, China again is just one such player.

China is motoring. It's getting richer and hungrier. Since 1998 China has accounted for nearly the entire increase in global consumption of major commodities such as copper, tin and aluminium. But China also needs to feed itself, clothe itself and, as discussed, fuel itself. All this requires vast amounts of grain, beef, cotton and oil, the very things Africa is poised to provide. What China so desperately needs, Africa has: tea in Kenya, coffee in Uganda, beef in Botswana, cashews in Mozambique, cotton in Mali, oil in Gabon – the list goes on and on and on. And, in addition, Africa also accounts for nearly half of the world's production of bauxite, chrome and diamonds, for more than half of its cocoa and platinum, and nearly three quarters of its cobalt.

Over recent decades, China has registered unprecedented rates of economic growth – to the point that, today, China is the world's third-largest economy. It has achieved the seemingly impossible – moving vast numbers of its people from the depths of poverty, decidedly into the ranks of the middle class. Yet the 300 million in China's rising middle class are just a fraction of its 1.2 billion population. As China's middle class continues to grow, so too will its appetite.

For Africa, this is a golden opportunity.

But, in 2008, Sino-African trade was a paltry 2 per cent of China's total; fortunately these numbers are growing. Between 1990 and 2000, trade between China and Africa grew by 450 per cent. From 2002 to 2003, it rose over 50 per cent to almost US$12 billion and then nearly quadrupled by 2007, jumping to US$45 billion. China is now the continent's third most important trading partner, behind the US and France, and ahead of the UK.

As with FDI, the impressive rise in trade between China and Africa has primarily been driven by China's voracious appetite for raw materials, and most notably oil. But, although oil and mining have dominated trade between the two continents, there are now welcome signs of diversification, such as agricultural commodities. Burkina Faso sends a third of its exports, almost all of which are cotton, to China, compared with virtually nothing in the mid-1990s.

The trade figures sound fantastic – doubling, tripling and even quadrupling; on paper it looks like a bonanza. But the reality is quite different. There are still too many African countries standing by the sidelines, unable or unwilling to capitalize on the obvious opportunity staring them in the face. A mere five oil- and mineral-exporting countries account for almost 90 per cent of Africa's exports to China (in order of importance, Angola, Sudan, Equatorial Guinea, Gabon and Mauritania); this at a time when China's demand for grain, meat (China's meat consumption has doubled in just three years) and other foodstuffs is rising at an unprecedented rate. With only 7 per cent of the world's arable land, and a billion-plus people to feed, China will have to shop everywhere. And it is doing everything it can in Africa to make up the numbers – offering duty-free treatment to some goods (increasing the number of tariff-free imports to over 400, from 190), establishing trade and economic cooperation zones, and going so far as to set up a China–Africa Joint Chamber of Commerce and Industry.

For some reason, many African countries seem to be reluctant to embrace this eager suitor. There are fears that an African fixation on trade with China, and catering to China's all-pervasive needs, will solidify the continent's status as only a commodity exporter, and history has shown that no country has become rich by relying on its agricultural exports alone (save, perhaps, New Zealand). But this is not about perfection; it's about survival – and survival today.

The theory would go that the trajectory of economic development starts with agricultural production (African states dominate this lowest rung of the economic ladder, mirrored by their lowest per capita incomes), moves up the curve to manufacturing (currently dominated by Asia), then services, ending up with high-value-added research and development (the latter two stages populated with the world's most economically rich and industrialized countries – the US, Singapore, Germany, etc.). And, obviously, it should be every country's dream to attain the highest income levels. But many of the most successful Asian countries have made the transition from commodity exporter to manufacturing powerhouse. The question is, what has happened to Africa?

While Asian economies were scaling the manufacturing ladder, African nations have (all but a few) been relegated to agricultural producers (but even so are sometimes unable to feed themselves). African labour is not more expensive than Asian labour – the converse is, in fact, true. On pure wages alone, Africa should dominate the world's manufacturing slot (manufacturing does tend to employ lowly skilled workers, so Africa's poor education showing ought not to hamper its prospects of becoming a manufacturing engine). But once the infrastructure costs are factored in, Africa is a let-down in spades.

Although Africa is the centre of the universe on the area-accurate Peters Projection Map (occupying a much-coveted proximity to the industrialized hubs of Europe and America), it takes way too long to transport goods on its unnavigable rivers, impassable bridges and pot-holed roads. Besides, to state the obvious, no profit-seeking company can afford to bet on Africa's unreliable power and erratic telecommunications as the source of its manufactured inputs. Of course, were Africa's dire infrastructure predicament remedied, its chance for higher-value trade (thereby distancing itself from the tag of commodity exporter) could dramatically improve. Thankfully, as discussed in Chapter 7, the recent foray into Africa by China and others means there is some hope that the infrastructure will be there for Africa to move up the development curve.

There are also concerns – given that trade works both ways – that Africa is susceptible to China flooding the markets with cheap manufactured goods. There is clearly the risk that cheaper Chinese goods can undercut African manufacturers, putting our mosquito net producer back out of business. He is definitely out of business in the aid scenario, and could be out of business in the Chinese trade scenario, but the important point here is much more nuanced. Crucially, under the aid regime there is nothing else for him to do – he lives in a sterile landscape, opportunities are scarce, and corruption is rife. In the trade scenario, even with a modicum of corruption, opportunities abound – there is a thriving economy, people are buying and selling. Our mosquito net producer, who's forced to stop making mosquito nets, might start making hair nets for a burgeoning middle class; or may in another way need to retool. The point is, as hardhearted as it sounds, it is better to face economic hardship in a thriving economy with prospects than to be confronted by it in an aid-dependent economy, where there are none. Mosquito man lives.

Dongo can benefit from trade

Dongo can clearly benefit from more trade – trade creates employment, improves trade balances, lowers the price of consumer goods through greater imports and generates income for the country's exporters, but, perhaps most importantly, trade produces income that accrues to governments through tariffs and income taxes.

However, common sense should tell Dongo that it would be foolhardy to hitch itself to China alone. Certainly Africa makes up only 2 per cent of China's trade, so obviously there is scope for expansion. But, equally, there is a lot of scope for Africa's trade partnerships to develop elsewhere, and although China has emerged as Africa's preeminent partner, it is by no means the only one.

India, too, is anxious to trade with Africa. Although the Indian Junior Commerce Minister, Jairam Ramesh, remarked that 'there is no race between us, the Chinese have left us far, far behind', Indo-African trade has risen from US$1 billion in 1991 to US$30 billion in 2007/2008.[6]

At the first India–Africa Forum, attended by eight African heads of state, calling for a 'new architecture' in the Indo-African partnership, India's Prime Minister, Manmohan Singh, announced dutyfree access to Indian markets for the world's fifty least-developed countries (LDC), thirty-four of which are African. India has pledged preferential market access on 92.5 per cent of all LDC exports, including diamonds, cotton, cocoa, aluminium ore and copper ore.

In just five years (since 2003), African trade to Asia has grown by almost 30 per cent a year.

According to the World Bank economist Harry G. Broadman, 'skyrocketing' Afro-Asian trade represents the beginning of a change in trade patterns. Although most trade is still between Africa and Europe, Japan or North America, Broadman notes: 'what's going on in China, India, and Africa is part of the broader trend in the world of rapidly growing South–South investment and trade – trade among developing countries'.

But, like charity, trade begins at home. Africa need not look so far away: it can look to itself. Although since the 1970s there has been a proliferation of economic and trade agreements – the Preferential Trade Agreement, Common Market for Eastern and Southern Africa, Southern Africa Development Community, Economic Community of West African States, East African Community and, recently, New Partnership for Africa's Development – most of these agreements have had a lot of bark but very little bite. No doubt political intransigence and myopia have once again prevailed.

There are numerous policies the African leadership should seriously embrace to boost trade and increase regional cohesiveness
and integration. A simple decree to remove inter-country trade
barriers, which average more than 30 per cent, would be a good
start. It is bizarre that shipping a car from Japan to Abidjan, in
Ivory Coast, costs US$1,500, whereas moving it from Abidjan to
Addis Ababa, in Ethiopia, costs US$5,000.[7]

African leaders must also take a broader view on what a trading
market means. There are 10 million people in Zambia, but 150
million in the Southern African region alone. Similarly, Kenya has
almost 40 million people, but with Uganda and Tanzania the East
African market is about 100 million. How much more economically (and politically) powerful these regions would be if leaders
learnt to think big. One day soon, hopefully, Dongo could become
part of a free-trade, single-currency, vibrant economic zone –
think America, think European Union. But also think East Asian
Miracle, where regional integration such as the Association of
Southeast Asian Nations played a vital role in ensuring the region's
startling success.

Trade is not the panacea of Africa's woes – but with the prospect
of US$100 billion in trade income each year from China alone, it
is bound to put a dent in them.

Trade need not just be international. Take a country like Pakistan, for example. With little trade to show (Pakistan's trade share
of GDP in 2006 was only 37 per cent – less than half the low-
income group mean trade openness ratio), it has registered solid
growth rates – in 2006, Pakistan's GDP growth was around 7 per
cent. How has it done this? The simple answer is, by generating
domestic demand for goods and services locally produced (that is,
its non-tradeable sector).

African countries must also focus on their non-tradeable sector
by encouraging their entrepreneurs (of course, FDI can boost
the non-tradeable sector also). The entrepreneurs (their small and
medium-sized enterprises) are the life-blood of any economy, and
the crucial emerging private sector in poor countries is the engine
for private-sector-led growth. Yet, although small and medium

enterprises (SMEs) are a significant part of the total employment in the most developed and rapidly developing countries, their share across African economies (rather disturbingly given the abundance of labour) lags behind. Whereas SMEs (defined as formal-sector enterprises with up to 250 employees) account for as much as 60 per cent across countries like Japan, Denmark and Ireland (and more than 80 per cent in Italy and Greece), Zambia's share of SMEs is 40 per cent, and Cameroon's just 20 per cent. If these two African countries are anything to go by there is clearly much scope for improvement across the board.

Entrepreneurs need a receptive and user-friendly environment within which to thrive, but they also need money. Entrepreneurial firms are more likely to spring up in countries where there is better access to finance (as well as business environments where it's easier to do business). Fortunately, there are other non-aid ways to finance themselves and contribute to their countries' development.

9. Banking on the Unbankable

In December 2006, Muhammad Yunus, a Bangladeshi national, was awarded the Nobel Peace Prize.[1] His work on structuring financing in Bangladesh revolutionized the thinking on how to lend to the poorest, and most rural, segments of countries; that is, the communities in which the majority of poor people are employed in the agricultural sector, often buffeted by unpredictable events, and live in villages which lack physical infrastructure (roads or power supplies), making the costs of establishing a formal banking network prohibitive.

Professor Yunus's innovation was to find a way to lend to the poorest of the poor who have no collateral – no house, no car, no tangible asset against which to borrow. People whose only nominal personal wealth would probably be in the form of land, where the collateral is undocumented and legally unenforceable.

Looking across Bangladesh, Yunus realized that although many villages had no obvious visible asset, they all shared one thing – a community of interdependence and trust. The genius behind Yunus's Grameen Bank (literally translated from Bengali as 'Bank of the Village') was in converting that trust into collateral.[2]

The mechanics of Grameen Bank's solidarity lending are pretty straightforward. Take a small village with five traders for a basic illustration. Through its micro-lending programme, the Grameen Bank lends the group US$100. Within the group the US$100 is passed on to trader A for a pre-specified period (a loan period currently runs for about one year). At the end of this time, she (97 per cent of Grameen's loans are made to women) has to pay back to Grameen Bank the loan amount plus interest (which can be between 8 and 12 per cent). Trader A is solely responsible for repaying her loan. When the loan is repaid, the next US$100 loan is made to the group, which is then passed on to trader B.

But if trader A does not repay, the group is extended no further loans.

Although, technically speaking, there is no group joint liability (the group as a whole is not responsible for the loan when one member defaults), the group *is* implicitly liable in the sense that the behaviour of each individual member affects the group as a whole. So very often when difficulties in repayment do arise, the group members contribute the defaulted amount (with an intention of collecting the money from the defaulted member at a later time), thus keeping the loan–cycle turning. In this sense micro-finance in poor countries works much like credit cards in rich countries – borrowers repay their loans because they know that if they don't pay the loans they have today, their lender will blacklist them, and they won't be able to borrow more tomorrow. The bonds of trust extend not only between the members of the group, but also between the group and the bank – there is no legal instrument between Grameen Bank and its borrowers.

The Grameen model has met with resounding success. At least forty-three countries around the world have adopted some version of it. Grameen Bank initially offered micro-finance to 36,000 members with a portfolio of US$3.1 million when it became a bank in 1983. By 1997, it had 2.3 million members and a portfolio of US$230 million. Perhaps most impressively, its default rates are at less than 2 per cent and, with its success, the bank now provides a host of other financial services (beyond also insurance and pension schemes) to the poor – micro-enterprise, scholarships and housing programmes.

According to Grameen Bank estimates from March 2008, over 1.3 million members took micro-enterprise loans (mainly for power-tillers, irrigation pumps, motor vehicles, and river craft for transportation and fishing), for a total of over US$450 million. On the education side, scholarships amounting to US$950,000 have been awarded to over 50,000 children, and by March 2008 nearly 23,000 students received higher-education loans, many for medicine, engineering and professional certificates. Finally, in the twelve months to February 2008, Grameen housing loans alone have reached US$1.19 million with some 8,300 houses having been built. Since the housing programme's inception in 1984, over 650,000 houses have been constructed.

The most truly extraordinary aspect of this extraordinary tale is their 'No Donor Money, No Loans' policy. In 1995, Grameen Bank decided not to receive any more donor funds, and today funds itself 100 per cent through its deposits. Although recognized as the grandfather of micro-credit and micro-lending, Grameen Bank has spawned numerous variations all over the world, all targeting the segment of the population that has fallen through the high-street banking cracks. The BKI in Indonesia, Acción in Latin America, BRAC in Bangladesh and K-REP in Kenya are just a sample of the growing and expansive list.

In Africa, Zambia offers an interesting case study of how micro-finance has developed. Traditionally, conservative banking institutions have generally targeted large and established companies (for example, those in the mining sector) and shown little appetite for small businesses and individuals (save a few high-income salaried earners). In a population of around 10 million people, where only about 500,000 are formally employed, some 9.5 million (although this includes children) remained ignored by the banking sector. Enter micro-finance. The many thousands of would-be Zambian entrepreneurs finally had a way to secure capital to fund their businesses.

In practice, like many other poor countries, the Zambian micro-finance market can be split into three tiers. The first two target salaried workers, who pay different rates of interest depending on their employer. In the first tier are civil servants (doctors, teachers and military personnel), who by virtue of working for the government are charged relatively low interest rates. Second come salaried professionals, not employed by government (lawyers and bankers) and who, because they work in the private sector and do not have the security of the government behind them, are charged a higher rate of interest. In each of these two cases, the micro-loan lender uses the salary as collateral – using the individuals' wage to directly secure the loan.

The third category, which encompasses the vast majority of Zambia's poor, and for which the Grameen Bank structure was originally intended, are the unsalaried, often rural poor, with variable incomes, and generally no access to loan capital – think of a woman selling tomatoes on a side street. Yet this group – the real entrepreneurs, the backbone of Zambia's economic future – need capital just as much as the mining company to see their businesses established and grow.

In Zambia, as in other African countries where micro-finance has started to blossom, the risk of lending to the most risky is often reduced through joint liability – the notion that members of a group of borrowers are *all* liable for any loans that a micro-finance lender makes to them.

Consider again a group of borrowers in a small rural village, where the lender has virtually no information on the individual borrowers. Joint liability gets around this information asymmetry in a number of ways. When forming their groups, borrowers have an incentive at the onset to match themselves with other good borrowers, and exclude those known to be high-risk. Naturally, this self-selection mechanism helps the lender screen the borrowers and reduce the risk of default. Joint liability also addresses the moral hazard lenders typically face – that is, the risk that once a loan is made, once the borrower has secured the cash, she defaults. Under joint liability, other members of the group have a vested interest to ensure their partners do not cheat, to see the loan repaid, so that they too can access funds.

Having seen the explosion and success in micro-finance (micro-finance default rates in Zambia are less than 5 per cent), traditional banks have woken up to the opportunity that hitherto they have left untapped. Since 2000, there has been a rapid growth in international investment in micro-lending by various agencies and funds that tend to be more commercially oriented. By mid-2004, this group had invested a total of nearly US$23 billion in about 450 micro-finance institutions.

But micro-finance is not without its naysayers. This type of lending to the poor is criticized as loan-sharking (charging punitive and exorbitant rates), as fuelling Ponzi schemes (borrowing from one lender to pay off another) and as simply supporting reckless consumption. However, with ever-increasing numbers of micro-lenders, and growing participation in this type of lending, the interest rates charged inevitably become lower and, in this sense, more competitive. As to the Ponzi scheme criticism, the objection merely points to the need for more information concerning borrowers – who's good and who's bad (which, by the way, is exactly the information asymmetry that the Grameen model mitigates). And on the issue of consumption versus investment, this applies to any loan, any time, anywhere.

The important point, not to be overlooked, is that the previously unbankable and excluded poor are now part of a functioning financial dynamic. With this comes a culture of borrowing and repayment crucial for financial development in a well-oiled successful economy. Small-scale banking to poor people has the capacity to create enterprise and growth in developing countries.

Lending to the poor is also no longer constrained by national boundaries, or by financial institutions. With the advent of Kiva, a California-based interface, pretty much anyone sitting anywhere with a keyboard can lend money to anyone across the planet.[3] This is how it works: a woman in Cameroon goes on line seeking a US$200 loan towards her tailoring business. She makes her case, as best she can, and a man in Des Moines, Iowa, lends her US$25 of it, someone in Sweden lends another US$25, and the balance is covered by someone in Japan. The loan is made for a set period, for a pre-agreed interest rate, and she regularly updates her lenders on her progress. In the week – just one week – leading into 19 April 2008, over US$625,000 was lent by almost 3,000 new lenders.

Like the Grameen model (and unlike aid) the default rates have been minimal. Thus far, since Kiva's inception in 2005, some US$30 million has been lent, 45,000 loans made to people in forty-two countries. A wonderful innovation – get involved.

Remember the mosquito net manufacturer who, thanks to aid, is now out of business? And remember the 176 people (one owner, ten workers and their 165 dependants) now with no stable income, dependent on handouts?

How much better would it have been if just half of the million-dollar donation had been invested as micro-lending in the country instead? Within five years, our mosquito net manufacturer could have expanded production to meet growing demand, doubled his workforce (and by default provided support for another 150 of their dependants), and his product would be there to replace the nets as they fell into disrepair.

Of course, other entrepreneurs, seeing how his business has flourished and recognizing the ever-present demand for mosquito nets, would venture into the market, thereby lowering the cost of the nets over time, and of course improving quality.

What should Dongo do?

The extension of financial services to people who otherwise have no access to banks dates as far back as when municipal savings banks began in Europe in the eighteenth century, and when German groups based on the self-help principle and called savings and credit cooperatives were first organized by Herman Schulze-Delitzsch and Friedrich Raiffeisen in the middle of the nineteenth century.

In more recent times, micro-credit organizations were developed in the 1960s to serve Africa and Asia's needs for agricultural support, yet most Africans today still have very limited access to financial markets. In Ghana and Tanzania, for example, only about 5–6 per cent of the population has access to the banking sector, although some 80 per cent of households in Tanzania would be prepared to save if they had access to appropriate products and saving mechanisms.

The oldest private, worldwide, fully commercial micro-finance investment fund is the Dexia Micro-Credit Fund. It is managed by Blue Orchard Finance, a micro-finance investment consultancy, and finances some fifty micro-finance institutions in twenty-four countries. It has investments of US$77 million. However, it was really not until Grameen Bank's success that micro-finance really took off.

Today, micro-finance brings groups of people into the economy for the first time, by offering the poor a range of saving tools. Beyond the direct capital injection it puts into a borrower's pockets, it can also be a powerful development tool. Even small loans can boost business productivity gains and contribute to job creation and raise family living standards (better nutrition, better health and housing, more education).

By some estimates some 10,000 organizations (from non-governmental organizations to registered banks) today offer over US$1 billion worth of micro-finance loans annually to many millions of customers around the world; projections are that this amount will have to grow twenty-fold (to US$20 billion) over the next five years to meet projected demand. But in more extreme forecasts, some predict even more exponential growth. Vijay Mahajan, a micro-finance practitioner, puts potential annual micro-credit demand in India alone at US$30 billion, 10 per cent of the estimated global US$300 billion.[4] According to an April 2006 survey by McKinsey Consulting, India has the potential to become a US$500 billion market by the year 2020.

Growth in most emerging-market regions has been meteoric: For example, the Bangladeshi organization BRAC signed up 5,000 customers in Afghanistan, just six months after setting up there; two Cambodian organizations (Acleda and EMT) each have over 80,000 customers; Banco do Nordeste in Brazil has become the second-largest micro-finance operation in Latin America, with 110,000 clients in just a few years; and Compartamos, in Mexico, has nearly doubled the number of its clients in the past year to become the largest Latin American programme, with over 150,000 clients.

Despite all this expansion, the industry has yet to reach 5 per cent of the customers among the world poor. Even according to the Grameen Foundation USA's more optimistic estimates that 10 per cent of a potential US$300 billion micro-finance market has been penetrated, there is plenty of scope for development financing through micro-lending. It's about time Dongo, and the rest of Africa, got involved.

Remittances

The UN estimates that there are around 33 million Africans living outside their country of origin. Nigerians and Ghanaians principally move to the United States, Malians and Senegalese settle in France, and the majority of Congolese make their home in the Netherlands. Some 30 per cent of Mali's population lives elsewhere. In total, emigrants represent almost 5 per cent of Africa's total population, and they are yet another source of money to help fuel Africa's development.

Remittances – the money Africans abroad sent home to their families – totalled around US$20 billion in 2006 (remittances were US$68 billion and US$113 billion in Latin America and Asia, respectively). According to a United Nations report entitled *Resource Flows to Africa: An Update on Statistical Trends*, between 2000 and 2003 Africans sent home about US$17 billion each year, a figure that even tops FDI, which averaged US$15 billion, during this period. What is more, according to the World Bank, the figures on Africa's remittances are most likely grossly undervalued, as a lot of money makes its way to the continent through unrecorded channels (Freund and Spatafora estimate informal remittances are 35–75 per cent of the official flows); so much so that remittances may possibly be the largest source of external funding in many poor countries. At US$5 billion, Nigeria receives the greatest amount of remittances in Africa, followed by South Africa (US$1.5 billion) and Angola (US$1 billion). They accounted for roughly 40 per cent of Somalia's 2006 GDP, the same year that six out of fifty-three countries received remittances in excess of US$1 billion. Quite clearly remittances are (and increasingly should be) a significant piece of many African countries' financing puzzle.

In July 2006, the UK's Department of International Development published a report, *The Black and Minority Ethnic Remittance Survey*, which revealed that within black communities 34 per cent of Africans send money home to relatives. Perhaps more startling

was the fact that of the almost 10,000 minority households inter-
viewed across the UK, Black Africans were found to remit money
(an average of around £910 annually, or almost US$1,800; the
global average per capita is around US$200 per month) more
frequently than any other group.

Like the other forms of private capital flows already discussed,
the benefits of remittances are far-reaching.

Although the actual remittance sums taken individually are relatively small, taken collectively the remittance amounts flowing
into African nations' coffers (banks, building societies, etc.) are
enormous. The US$565 million that flowed into Mozambique and
the US$642 million that went to Uganda in 2006 most certainly
contributed to bolstering their economies.

Remittances can play an important part in financing a country's
external balances, by helping to pay for imports and repay external
debt. As remittances tend to be more stable than other capital
flows, in some countries banks have used them to securitize loans
from the international capital markets – that is, to raise overseas
financing using future remittances as collateral, thereby lowering
borrowing costs. Banco do Brasil raised US$250 million in 2002
by using future dollar- or yen-denominated worker remittances as
collateral.

An April 2008 World Bank publication entitled 'Beyond Aid:
New Sources and Innovative Mechanisms for Financing Development in Sub-Saharan Africa', estimated that sub-Saharan African
countries can potentially raise as much as US$1–3 billion by reduc-
ing the cost of international migrant remittances, US$5–10 billion
by issuing diaspora bonds (a bond issued by a country (or even a
private company) to raise financing from its overseas diaspora), and
US$17 billion by securitizing future remittances – not small
change. Incidentally, India and Israel have raised as much as US$11
billion and US$25 billion, respectively, from their diaspora abroad,
showing that these schemes can work, and work very well if
executed efficiently.[5]

On a household level, remittances are used to finance basic
consumption needs: housing, children's education, healthcare, and

even capital for small businesses and entrepreneurial activities – the heart of an economy. More fundamentally, more remittances mean more money deposited in the bank, which means more cash that the banks have to lend. In Latin America, deposits-to-GDP ratios (a key indicator of a country's financial development) markedly improved as a result of high remittances. Naturally, the most direct channel through which remittances have an impact on GDP is by increased spending by the recipient households.

Remittances make an important and growing contribution to relieving poverty. According to a paper by World Bank economists, evidence shows that a 10 per cent increase in per capita remittances leads to a 3.5 per cent decline in the proportion of poor people. Household surveys in the Philippines indicate that a 10 per cent increase in remittances reduced the poverty rate by 2.8 per cent by increasing the income level of the receiving family but also via spillovers to the overall economy. Moreover, this 10 per cent increase led to a 1.7 per cent increase in school attendance, a 0.35-hour decline in child labour per household per week, and a 2 per cent increase in new entrepreneurial activities.[6]

All of this is good news, but there is a price to be paid – and one that potentially constrains the growth of remittances to the continent. For every US$100 sent to Africa, only US$80 gets there – the middleman takes the rest – while from the US to Mexico US$85 gets home (that is, a 15 per cent charge), and from the UK to India as much as US$96 (just a 4 per cent tax) reaches its destination.

This form of higher 'taxation' on monies sent to Africa throws up a double-whammy: it encourages those abroad to send money secretly and can ultimately discourage them from sending any money at all. In a survey, remitters said that they would send 10 per cent more money if costs were 50 per cent cheaper.

The bulk of the transfer cost for remitting money from the sender abroad to the recipient at home is determined in the private markets. Therefore, the high remittance costs can really only be reduced by increasing access to banking and strengthening competition in the remittance industry.

However, there is scope for African governments to encourage greater remittance flows by offering cheaper ways for money to be sent home. In Latin America, for example, the International Remittance Network facilitates remittance flows from the United States to Latin America. Similar initiatives in Africa would undoubtedly do the same. It is encouraging to note that innovative mobile phone technology is making it both cheaper and quicker for people to send and receive money. In April 2007, a money transfer system called M-Pesa was launched in Kenya enabling subscribers to send large sums of money in an instant transaction. Within just two weeks of the launch over 10,000 account holders were registered and more than US$100,000 had been transferred. At the moment the M-Pesa programme only facilitates money transfers within the country's borders, usually from richer urban dwellers to their poorer rural relations. However, there are plans underway to roll the scheme out on an international basis, not only tapping the billions of international remittances Kenyans regularly send home, but doing it in the most competitive way – that is, getting more cash into the recipient's pocket.

Remittances are, of course, in some sense a form of aid (the recipient is essentially getting something for nothing). And like other forms of aid, there is the inherent risk that remittances encourage reckless consumption and laziness. In 2006, Jamaica's finance minister, Dr Omar Davies, expressed concern that the multimillion-dollar flows of remittances to Jamaicans were instilling a culture of dependency over achievement.

Perhaps this is true, but at least some part of the money is reaching the indigent and making its way to productive uses. And unlike aid it does not increase corruption. Indeed, Giuliano and Ruiz-Arranz, and Toxopeus and Lensink, conclude that remittances do have a positive impact on growth.

Savings

In April 2005, two young boys stumbled upon US$6,000 while playing football in Maiduguri, in north-east Nigeria. Maiduguri is not Nigeria's bustling capital city of Abuja or its largest commercial city of Lagos; nor, for that matter, is it Nigeria's third, fourth or fifth business hubs (those honours go to Port Harcourt, Kano and Ibadan). Yet it was here, in Maiduguri, that the US$6,000 was found.[7]

This money hadn't been lost. As it turns out, in the absence of a credible, formalized banking system the owner of the cash had opted to neatly wrap his savings in a black plastic bag and hide his stash near a rubbish dump.

This incident raises a fundamental question: does Africa lack capital? Or might it be that there is a lot of cash in these poor countries – unseen, dormant cash, which simply needs to be woken? Could it actually be that the countless development agents and agencies and innumerable man-hours deployed to send cash to Africa have been for naught – attempting to address a problem that simply does not exist? That, in fact, the core problem with Africa is not an absence of cash, but rather that its financial markets are acutely inefficient – borrowers cannot borrow, and lenders do not lend, despite the billions washing about.

In *The Mystery of Capital*, the Peruvian economist Hernando de Soto suggests that the value of savings among the poor of Asia, the Middle East and Africa is as much as forty times all the foreign aid received throughout the world since 1945. He argues that were the United States to hike its foreign-aid allocations to the 0.7 per cent of national income (as prescribed by the United Nations at Monterrey), it would take the richest country more than 150 years to transfer to the world's poor resources equal to those that they already have.

Evidence from India would seem to add weight to this theory. By some estimates, as much as US$200 billion worth of untapped investment potential is privately held in gold in India.[8] In 2005,

India introduced a policy which allowed Indians to exchange their physical gold holdings (often held in jewellery and coins) into 'paper' gold in denominations as low as US$2. Estimates suggest that this policy unlocked as much as US$200 billion worth of untapped investment potential privately held. The initiative promised to bring the poorest 700 million villagers, who purchase about two thirds of India's gold, into the more formalized banking system. Moreover, this gold policy injected more money into the economy than the total FDI India received in 2004 – in that year Indians poured about twice as much money into gold (around US$10 billion) as the country received from foreign investors. With more than half of India's savings tied up in physical assets, such strategies can bring millions of poor into the banking system, offering credit access to many Indians, and inject capital into the economy.

The Indian experience is an example of how a government has successfully unlocked latent resources. Africa should take note and look for ways to bring the hidden money into the financial stream. Of course, Africans might not hoard gold to the same extent as Indians, but many of them do have access to (and nominal ownership of) the land they till. And this is de Soto's main argument, that the inability of people across the developing world to secure their property rights is what prevents them from unlocking their vast capital. What is needed is a functioning and transparent legal framework so that Africans can convert that land into collateral against which they can borrow and invest.

It is not the case that African countries do not have legal frameworks (many inherited from their colonial past); it is, however, the case that in environments of rampant corruption the legal systems are often impotent.

Savings are a hugely important part of a country's growth, and a country's financial development. Domestic saving is the most important source of financing investment and thus boosting growth. Looking back at the Grameen Bank model, it too includes a component to encourage saving amongst its borrowers – in fact, they are required to save and invest. Customers must save US$0.02 per week, and new members are required to buy a share of stock in Grameen for US$2; localized financial development at its best.

What Africa desperately needs is more innovation in the financial sector. We can put a man on the moon, so we can most certainly crack Africa's financing puzzle, jump-start economic growth and drastically reduce poverty. But herein lies the key – innovation. Innovation means breaking out of the mould, and finding more-applicable ways for Africa to finance its development. There is a history of financial innovation to draw from: the Soft Banks of America's Wild West and the Scottish Banks of the eighteenth century. Both catered to the unsecured and traditionally unbankable.

At the time of the gold rush in 1800s California, for example, one would have expected the well-established East Coast American banks to have simply migrated westwards, opening branches and setting up their lending shops on the West Coast to cater to the demand from those in search of yellow (and black) gold. Instead, what happened was that there emerged hybrid banking structures – a combination of venture capital, where the lenders would lend money with the prospect of a portion of the spoils when the borrower struck gold, and standard lending practices, where the borrower would have to pay back the principal plus some interest (in this case the lender got no share in the project). To illustrate, under a venture capital (VC) arrangement, the lender would give the collateral-less gold-seeker US$1,000 to invest in exploration and hiring all the staff he needed, and in return the lender would get 20 per cent of the gold project or all future profits emanating from the project. Naturally, this structure was very different to the standard banking practices which would have lent out the US$1,000 with an interest rate attached. But, of course, under standard banking practices most of the borrowers without collateral would have been excluded. In essence, as is the case in many places in Africa today, the gold-rushers of America's Wild West had a good idea, but no collateral which standard bankers would feel happy to lend against.

The financing revolution of eighteenth-century Scotland was not much different in its innovative thinking. By essentially becoming a fully fledged, all-service financial supermarket (providing all elements of banking – venture capital, standard commercial banking, investment banking, merchant banking, etc.), Scottish banks could customize the cash and liquidity needs of a whole range of businesses and individual entrepreneurs. Banking and finance are about risk – risk assessment, risk mitigation and risk estimation. Scottish financial engineers had figured it out. Even if a potential borrower did not meet a bank's standard, prescribed risk profile (that is, had no collateral, no guarantees, no obvious ability to repay), rather than turn them away the bank would tailor a lending instrument to meet the risk profile of the borrower. Certainly, it might have meant infinite permutations to get the right structure, but there was never any doubt that a financing structure could be found.

There is a story, for example, of how two independent farm owners each applied for financing to invest in their individual farms. The lender could not see how to lend to each farm individually, but somehow if the two farms were merged, their risks pooled, and therefore mitigated, a loan arrangement could be struck.

It is this type of innovation, providing micro-loans as well offering hybrid venture capital structures (in addition to standard banking fare), that Africa should look to replicate in order to bring its masses into the global fold. No country has economically succeeded without finding a way to funnel the risk capital to finance its small and medium-sized enterprises. For Africa, this is an imperative that must be heeded.

Dongo Revisited

After sixty years of dead aid, Dongo is regressing. Its finances stand as follows: roughly 75 per cent of the money coming into the economy is from foreign aid (essentially, all of which accrues to the government), capital markets 3 per cent, trade 5 per cent, foreign direct investment (including micro-finance) 5 per cent, and the rest from remittances and savings. This financing portfolio has been costly, and Dongo is going nowhere fast.

If Dongo is to survive, development finance demands a new way of thinking. It needs to abandon the obsession with aid and draw on proven financial solutions. Dongo should aim for just 5 per cent of its total development financing to come from aid, 30 per cent from trade (with China as the lead partner), 30 per cent from FDI, 10 per cent from the capital markets, and the 25 per cent that is left should emanate from remittances and harnessed domestic savings. The key is to wean countries off aid by putting them on a tight schedule instead of continuing to give them open-ended commitments.

Clearly, however, not all African countries are equal, and what might be right for Dongo may not be suitable for land-locked Zambia, Zimbabwe and Chad, versus oil-rich Sudan, Nigeria and Angola. But the point is that, in order to succeed and escape the mire of poverty and despair, they need a mix of each of these solutions and an end to aid-dependency.

It has been shown, from case to case and example to example, that this can be done. In fact, in many African countries some of this is already being done, but on nowhere near the scale that is needed. Implementation (as we shall see) will be challenging, but not impossible.

The transition from today's low equilibrium to tomorrow's economic promise requires proper and active management, as challenges will inevitably arise. As described earlier, large capital inflows, whatever the source, can introduce the risk of Dutch disease (although Rajan and Subramanian have found no evidence that remittances hurt export competitiveness). But where private capital trumps aid every time is on the question of governance. You can steal aid every day of the week, whereas with private capital you only get one shot. If you steal the cash proceeds of an international bond issue, you most certainly will not be able to get more cash this way. The capital markets may be forgiving, but not so forgiving as to be fooled by the same culprit twice. And without cash to assuage the restlessness of an army, no despot can stand.

Besides, whereas earnings from trade filter through to many thousands of exporters and remittances accrue to innumerable households, foreign aid almost exclusively lands up in the hands of a 'lucky' few. Quite simply, investment money is not as easy to steal.

Africa's time is now. In the past five years there has been good economic and political news from the continent. Helped, in part, by soaring commodity prices, African countries are posting solid growth numbers, and, although nascent, positive political changes have swept across the continent. But these will count for little if the proposals set out here, essential for Africa's growth trajectory, are not implemented. Opportunities abound; investment prospects lie all around, in every sector – agriculture, telecommunications, power, infrastructure, banking and finance, retail, property. How can they not? With roughly a billion people Africa is a big continent. This continent needs everything: roads, hospitals, schools, airports, food, houses, cars, trains, aeroplanes. There is inordinate demand, and supply is not coping.

In the near term, external forces like the Chinese can and should play a key role in jump-starting Africa's renaissance. But African countries would be wise to prepare for the eventuality that China could pack up and leave – Africa may not always be the belle of the ball. Countries must after all face up to the reality that circumstances change – their resource endowments are not infinite, and commodity prices could tumble from the highs of today; but the good news is that some countries are already hedging against this possibility by saving their commodity windfalls.

The *Dead Aid* strategies, if embraced wholeheartedly, will not only turn the economic tide in the short term, but also promise longer-term growth. And as the growth pie expands, so too does a country's tax base – another reliable source of development finance.

Good governance trumps all. In a world of bad governance the cost of doing business is much higher, on every level. This is true even when investments are securitized (that is, backed by a specific asset), since the risk premium associated with the unpredictable behaviour of a bad government always looms large. As long as issues of bad governance linger overhead (guaranteed to be the case in a world of aid-dependency), the cost of investing in Africa will always be exorbitantly high even when the social benefits (such as skill transfer, education and infrastructure) are taken into account. Yet in a world of good governance, which will naturally emerge in the absence of the glut of aid, the cost (risk) of doing business in Africa will be lower (whether the investment is securitized or not).

The absolute imperative to make Africa's positive growth trajectory stick is to rid the continent of aid-dependency, which has hindered good governance for so long.

10. Making Development Happen

It's time to stop pretending that the aid-based development model currently in place will generate sustained economic growth in the world's poorest countries. It will not.

The question is how do we get African countries to abandon foreign aid and embrace the *Dead Aid* proposal? They can do it voluntarily – as South Africa or Botswana have done – but what if they don't, choosing the soft option of aid instead?

Let's step back a bit. Recall the August 1982 phone call when the Mexican Finance Minister telephoned the IMF, the US Treasury, et al. to inform them that Mexico would be unable to pay its debt. What if, in Africa's case, the scene were reversed?

What if, one by one, African countries each received a phone call (agreed upon by all their major aid donors – the World Bank, Western countries, etc.), telling them that in exactly five years the aid taps would be shut off – permanently? Although exceptions would be made for isolated emergency relief such as famine and natural disasters, aid would no longer attempt to address Africa's generic economic plight.

What would happen?

Would many more millions in Africa die from poverty and hunger? Probably not – the reality is that Africa's poverty-stricken don't see the aid flows anyway. Would there be more wars, more coups, more despots? Doubtful – without aid, you are taking away a big incentive for conflict. Would roads, schools and hospitals cease being built? Unlikely.

What do you think Africans would do if aid were stopped, simply carry on as usual? Too many African countries have already hit rock bottom – ungoverned, poverty-stricken, and lagging further and further behind the rest of the world each day; there is nowhere further down to go.

Isn't it more likely that in a world freed of aid, economic life for the majority of Africans might actually improve, that corruption would fall, entrepreneurs would rise, and Africa's growth engine would start chugging? This is the most probable outcome – that where the real chance exists to make a better life for themselves, their children and Africa's future generations, Africans would grab it and go.

If other countries around the developing world have done it *sans* aid (generated consistent growth, raised incomes and rescued billions from the brink of poverty), why not Africa? Remember that just thirty years ago Malawi, Burundi and Burkina Faso were economically ahead of China on a per capita income basis. A dramatic turnaround is always possible.

Grasping the nettle

How do we put the *Dead Aid* proposals into practice, and help to ensure that Africa gains a firm economic footing? There are three interlinked stages after the phone call.

First comes an economic plan which reduces a country's reliance on aid year on year. In Dongo's case, aid would fall 14 per cent every year – taking it down from the 75 per cent of income it receives today to 5 per cent in five years' time. For the first year, instead of 75 per cent, Dongo is now getting only 61 per cent of its income from aid. It now has to find the extra 14 per cent of money it requires from other *Dead Aid* means. In the second year, Dongo will have to find 28 per cent of its financial capital outside aid, and the year following, 42 per cent – nearly half of its needs.

We have offered an array of financing alternatives: trade, FDI, the capital markets, remittances, micro-finance and savings. It should come as no surprise that the *Dead Aid* prescriptions are market-based, since no economic ideology other than one rooted in the movement of capital and competition has succeeded in getting the greatest numbers of people out of poverty, in the fastest time.

Ultimately, where a country goes for its cash depends on its particular circumstances. For example, trade-oriented commodity-driven economies such as Zambia, Kenya and Uganda (actually the majority of African countries) should look at boosting trade with China and other emerging nations. And certainly the fifteen African countries which have recently acquired credit ratings should consider following Gabon and Ghana's lead in drawing on the capital markets.

Once the financing plan is in place, and Dongo knows how much it has to find, it must enforce rules of prudence and not live beyond its means. Like a family whose income has fallen, Dongo has two choices. It can either cut back on its expenditure or raise funds elsewhere to support the same level of spending. One would hope that any cutbacks would be on the non-essential, frivolous items (palaces, private jets and shopping trips to the Champs-Elysées in Paris), rather than schools, hospitals and infrastructure. With different forms of financing, without the same opportunity for corruption, the provision of schools, hospitals and infrastructure will anyway become cheaper. But in order to sustain the same degree of spending, Dongo would need to tap other sources of income. Using the *Dead Aid* proposals, the channels of money available will not only help maintain the same level of spending, but will of themselves encourage economic growth and increase the taxable middle classes, thereby broadening Dongo's financial alternatives.

Of course, nothing can stop a bad government from using the new money for old tricks. Some African leaders have been notoriously susceptible to shopping trips (Grace Mugabe, wife of Zimbabwe's president, is known for a penchant for shopping at London's exclusive Harrods department store), and some may be tempted again. But whereas the open purse of aid permits them to do this every year, if they use the private cash of the *Dead Aid* proposal for such ends, they will only get away with it once. If, for instance, a government were to steal the proceeds of a bond, or impose punitive taxes on its exporters, lenders would never lend again, and exporters would stop exporting. Over time, the economic pie that could be eaten into would grow smaller and smaller – and ultimately shrink into oblivion. Indeed, one could argue that the reason why Zimbabwe's Mugabe has lasted so long is because he has been propped up by massive foreign aid receipts; it certainly isn't Zimbabwe's burgeoning economy – US$300 million in foreign aid was sent there in 2006. In fact, without aid, the likelihood is that Mugabe might have been long gone. And regarding FDI, the Chinese expect something in return. Even if 80 per cent of their cash transfer is stolen, they still require that roads be built and the commodity extracted. Having amounts stolen is nowhere near a perfect solution, but at least a part of the cash benefit must accrue to the country.

The third stage in the *Dead Aid* model is the strengthening of institutions. At the core of the *Dead Aid* proposal is accountability. Those charged with the responsibility of providing public goods and ensuring the transparency and health of an environment within which the private sector can flourish must be held accountable when they fail to deliver. This has been the aid model's Achilles heel.

In *The Wealth and Poverty of Nations*, David Landes suggests that 'the ideal growth and development' government would:

secure rights of private property, the better to encourage saving and investment; secure rights of personal liberty . . . against both the abuses of tyranny and . . . crime and corruption; enforce rights of contract . . . provide stable government . . . governed by publicly known rules . . . provide responsive government . . . provide honest government . . . [with] no rents to favour and position; provide moderate, efficient ungreedy government . . . to hold taxes down [and] reduce the government's claim on the social surplus.[1]

Yet this is not the world in which most Africans live. In their world of aid-dependence, governments have failed at all these tasks, and failed spectacularly.

But is all this as easy as it sounds? One phone call, and it all slots into place? Why not? Development is not a mystery; each of the elements of the _Dead Aid_ proposal has been tried and tested and yielded success – and governments and policymakers know it.

The aid regime has been in place (in one form or another) for sixty years and demonstrably failed to generate economic growth and alleviate poverty. Given that in no other sphere (business, politics) has such a poor record been allowed to persist, why has the phone call not been made?

Who will bell the cat?

The _Dead Aid_ proposal is dead easy to implement. What it needs, and what is lacking, is political will. Political incentives are stacked against making the call.

Western donors have an aid industry to feed, farmers to placate (vulnerable when trade barriers are removed), liberal constituencies with 'altruistic' intentions to allay, and, facing their own economic challenges, very little time to worry about Africa's demise. For the Western politician maintaining the status quo of aid, it is much easier just to sign a cheque.

For African leaders too there is no immediate incentive to abandon the aid model – apart, of course, from the obvious one that were they to do so their countries' economic position would quickly improve. To appreciate the economic prospects in a non-aid environment, however, requires a long-term and selfless vision, and not the myopia so many policymakers (at home and abroad) are afflicted with today.

Unfortunately, there are still only a handful of (African) policymakers critical of aid's dismal performance. In a September 2007 interview with _Time_ magazine, Rwanda's President Kagame commented:

Now, the question comes for our donors and partners: having spent so much money, what difference did it make? In the last 50 years, you've spent US$400 billion in aid to Africa. But what is there to show for it? And the donors should ask: what are we doing wrong, or, what are the people we are helping doing wrong? Obviously somebody's not getting something right. Otherwise, you'd have something to show for your money.

The donors have also made a lot of mistakes. Many times they have assumed they are the ones who know what countries in Africa need. They want to be the ones to choose where to put this money, to be the ones to run it, without any accountability. In other cases, they have simply associated with the wrong people and money gets lost and ends up in people's pockets. We should correct that.[2]

In a similar vein, Senegal's President Wade remarked in 2002: 'I've never seen a country develop itself through aid or credit. Countries that have developed – in Europe, America, Japan, Asian countries like Taiwan, Korea and Singapore – have all believed in free markets. There is no mystery there. Africa took the wrong road after independence.'[3] Indeed, now *is* the time to correct, and not be swayed by media hype and populist and ill-conceived banter.

Ordinary people across Africa, the millions who bear the brunt of the economic catastrophe, have an incentive to change the aid regime of course. They would, if they could – who wouldn't? But they eke out their existence under a veiled (and often not so veiled) threat of intimidation, punishment and even death. In order to overturn the state aid-dependency, Africans need the gritty defiance of the unknown man who stood against the Chinese tanks in Tiananmen Square in June 1989. But such rebellion carries enormous risk, and when pitted against the omnipotent state, more likely than not, will fail.

This leaves it to Western citizens. They have power, and could hold the key to reform. It was, after all, thanks to the 60,000 ordinary Americans who wrote to the US Congress laying out their desire for freer trade access for African countries that the AGOA was born.[4] It is this type of activism that is needed to help jump-start Africa's development agenda, and set it on the right track.

Aid came from the West (and continues to do so), and it's up to the West to take it back. Why have people in the West not demanded that something be done? It is, after all, their money being poured down the drain. Maybe some have, but it's nearly impossible to be heard above the hectoring din of the purveyors of the 'Africa's glass is half empty' view of this world.

They say that aid worked – that the true test of aid's success is that millions of other Africans would have died were it not for aid. We can never really know if this is true (though we do know for sure that countries that have not relied on aid, including those in Africa like South Africa and Botswana, have consistently done better), and this justification for aid is changing the rules of the game. Aid was not originally designed or intended to be a sticking-plaster solution simply aimed at keeping people alive. The goals of aid, as originally set out by the forefathers in the New Hampshire hotel all those years ago, were sustainable economic growth and poverty alleviation, and it is against these goals that aid's efficacy should be judged, and against these that it has spectacularly failed.

Is there a moral obligation for Western societies to help poor countries? Clearly morality claims hold sway, but surely one would expect Western moralizers to adopt policies which help those in need rather than hinder them in the long run and keep them in a perilous state of economic despair. One solution that the aid proselytizers could adopt would be an egalitarian approach to donor donations. Instead of writing out a single US$250 million cheque to a country's government, why not distribute the money equally among its population. So in a country of 10 million people (roughly the population of Zambia) each citizen would get US$25 – a tenth of Zambia's current per capita income. In line with the *Dead Aid* proposals, this would in effect be a remittance 'donor-style'.

Indefinite grant transfers, however dressed up, are not something *Dead Aid* favours, but one could envisage how such remittances could be part of an effective financing package were the notions of accountability and repayment incorporated.

It is worth pointing out that there has been some notable success with a concept known as 'conditional cash transfers'; these are cash payments (in a sense, bonuses) made to give the poor an incentive to perform tasks that could help them escape poverty (for example, good school attendance, working a certain number of hours, improving test scores, seeing a doctor). The idea of conditional cash transfers has met with much success in developing countries such as Brazil, Mexico, Nicaragua and Peru (a similar programme is now being tested in the boroughs of New York City). Studies show the schemes have been instrumental in decreasing malnutrition, increasing school attendance and decreasing child labour.[5]

The genius of conditional cash transfer programmes (certainly in the context of developing countries) is threefold: they circumvent the government (bureaucracy and corruption are averted); payments are made for actually doing something rather than for doing nothing, which has often been the case with aid (quite simply, if you don't meet certain standards of behaviour, do certain things, meet specified criteria, you don't get paid); and the money actually ends up in the hands of the people that truly need it. The scheme has met with a resounding success in developing countries, so why has this type of programme not been rolled out aggressively across Africa? It would seem the logical thing to do given the failure of government-to-government aid.

Leaving the question of morality aside, there are good reasons based on national interest for the West to help. In the fractured world of Iran, Iraq and Afghanistan, Africa's fragile and impoverished states are a natural haven for global terrorists. Porous borders, weak law enforcement and security institutions, plentiful and portable natural resources, disaffected populations, and conflict zones make perfect breeding grounds for all sorts of global terrorist organizations.

The four horses of Africa's apocalypse – corruption, disease, poverty and war – can easily ride across international borders, putting Westerners at just as much risk as Africans. Of course, stolen money sent to European bank accounts can fund terrorist activities; disease, poverty and war induce waves of disenfranchised refugees and unchecked immigration, which can place inordinate burdens on Western economies.

The West can choose to ignore all of this, but, like it or not, the Chinese are coming. And it is in Africa that their campaign for global dominance will be solidified. Economics comes first, and when they own the banks, the land and the resources across Africa, their crusade will be over. They will have won.

Whether or not Chinese domination is in the interest of the average African today is irrelevant. This is not to underestimate how much Africans care about freedom and rights – they do. But in the immediate term a woman in rural Dongo cares less about the risk to her democratic freedom in forty years' time than about putting food on her table tonight. China promises food on the table today, education for her children tomorrow and an infrastructure she can rely on to support her business in the foreseeable future.

The mistake the West made was giving something for nothing. The secret of China's success is that its foray into Africa is all business. The West sent aid to Africa and ultimately did not care about the outcome; this created a coterie of elites and, because the vast majority of people were excluded from wealth, political instability has ensued.

China, on the other hand, sends cash to Africa and demands returns. With returns Africans get jobs, get roads, get food, making more Africans better off, and (at least in the interim) the promise of some semblance of political stability. It is the economy that matters. Places like Singapore have shown that, even in the absence of democracy, peace prevails when the median citizen is economically better off. In Africa, the 2008 fracas in Kenya may have been much more protracted had the average Kenyan had a lesser stake and vested interest in the economy. The situation may have gone on for as long as it did because, like any other society, there are, unfortunately, always people at the fringe who have yet to become fully fledged economic stakeholders and garner the benefits of a growing economy. The China movement in Africa is on the march – the West ignores it at its own peril.

Is there a role for the staid development formulas and old institutions of yesteryear? Surely, not to help Africa truly achieve sustainable growth and alleviate poverty as has so often been claimed. To support Africa in achieving this goal requires severing the Faustian bargain of current aid-driven development policy, and doing away with the ossified policies (and processes) that reign supreme in today's development debate. Fortunately, there has been some, albeit slow, movement in the right direction. Perhaps heeding the proverbial writing on the wall, or fearing their growing irrelevance in the development game where they were once the protagonist, international organizations are changing their tune.

There is a push towards greater inclusion of perspectives (from technocrats and policymakers) from the emerging world in the upper echelons of development agencies – who better to help shape the direction of the new development path? In 2008, for instance, the World Bank elected Justin Lin Yifu to the position of Chief Economist (considered the number two job at the international economic institution), which until this point had been occupied only by Americans or Europeans.

And terms like public–private partnerships and private-capital solutions to development financing (such as debt capital markets and diaspora bonds) have seeped into the development vocabulary, placing greater emphasis on the role of the private sector and seemingly now questioning rather than merely perpetuating the existing development model. This is undoubtedly a good start. As are the billions of dollars of smart money (the hedge funds, the international banks, the private equity funds) now going to Africa. Africa's era of private capital is only now beginning, and this trend has to be nurtured in order for it to continue.

There is more (much more) that needs to be done to undo the ills that have gone before, to rectify what has been an unmitigated disaster, and to get Africa onto a solid economic footing. While international donors and organizations must be commended for shifting the development ideology from the bad economic policies of the 1970s (mainly statist) to the good market policies on the books today (introduced on the back of the Washington Consensus), we need to remind them that without the elimination of aid effective implementation of the new, better, development regime will remain shoddy, ineffectual and even disastrous.

Africa's development impasse demands a new level of consciousness, a greater degree of innovation, and a generous dose of honesty about what works and what does not as far as development is concerned. And one thing is for sure, depending on aid has not worked. Make the cycle stop.

The best time to plant a tree is twenty years ago.
The second-best time is now.

African proverb

Notes

Preface

1. For details of the Battle of Adowa see http://en.wikipedia.org/wiki/BattleofAdowa.

Introduction

1. The 2001 Labour Party Conference was held in the City of Brighton and Hove.

1. The Myth of Aid

1. Various UNAIDS reports on the global AIDS epidemic.
2. Freedom House: http://www.freedomhouse.org; and International Institute for Democracy and Electoral Assistance: http://www.idea.int/.
3. http://en.wikipedia.org/wiki/JSESecuritiesExchange; http://en.wikipedia.org/wiki/ZimbabweStockExchange.
4. In terms of Price/Earnings (essentially a measure of how much value investors predict in the future of African companies), African P/Es, at 15 times, have been roughly commensurate with the emerging economies' (Brazil, Russia, India and China) average of 19 times.
5. Data sources are various issues of the World Bank World Development Indicators.
6. Average child mortality for Africa is 142 per 1,000 under-fives (World Bank World Development Indicators, 2006).
7. The Africa Progress Panel said in 2007: 'In 2006, Africa's growth stood at 5.4 percent . . . far short of the 7 percent annual growth that needs to be sustained to make substantial inroads into poverty reduction.'

8. Using the International Peace Research Institute, Oslo's armed conflict dataset, civil war is defined as an internal or internationalized internal armed conflict with at least 1,000 deaths in a year.

9. 'The President's Emergency Plan for AIDS Relief: U.S. Five Year Global HIV/AIDS Strategy', at http://www.state.gov/s/gac/plan/c11652.htm.

2. A Brief History of Aid

1. The forty-four countries represented were Australia, Belgium, Bolivia, Brazil, Canada, Chile, China, Colombia, Costa Rica, Cuba, Czechoslovakia, Dominican Republic, Ecuador, Ethiopia, France, Greece, Guatemala, Haiti, Honduras, Iceland, India, Iran, Iraq, Liberia, Luxembourg, Mexico, The Netherlands, New Zealand, Nicaragua, Norway, Panama, Paraguay, Peru, Philippines, Poland, South Africa, USSR, United Kingdom, United States, Uruguay, Venezuela, and Yugoslavia: http://web.worldbank.org/WBSITE/EXTERNAL/EXTABOUTUS/EXTARCHIVES/0,,contentMDK:64054691~menuPK:64319211~pagePK:36726~piPK:36092~theSitePK:29506,00.html.

2. The Marshall Plan speech: http://www.oecd.org/document/10/0,3343,en26492011851876938111111,00.html.

3. Sturzenegger and Zettelmeyer, 'Sovereign Defaults and Debt Restructurings'.

4. Lienert, 'Civil Service Reform in Africa'.

5. Nellis, 'Privatisation in Africa'.

6. *New York Times*, 4 February 1987.

7. Meredith, *The State of Africa*.

8. Corruption ranking based on the Transparency International scores.

9. Democracy is correlated with levels of development, but it is less clear whether democracy has a causal impact on development. Studies on the impact of democracy on economic growth are cautious in their conclusions and suggest no direct link per se between democracy and development.

10. Interview with Rwanda's President Kagame, *Time*, September 2007, at http://www.time.com/time/magazine/article/0,9171,1666064,00.html.

11. From Brenthurst Foundation July 2007 Discussion Paper: 'Speech by His Excellency President Paul Kagame'.

3. Aid is Not Working

1. Details of the 1885 Berlin Conference: http://en.wikipedia.org/wiki/BerlinConference.

2. 'Institutions that provide dependable property rights, manage conflict, maintain law and order, and align economic incentives with social costs and benefits are the foundation of long-term growth. The quality of institutions is key: good institutions are those that provide public officials with the incentives to provide market-fostering public goods at least cost in terms of corruption and rent seeking. Petty corruption, uncertain property rights, and inadequate courts are the source of problems': Rodrik, *In Search of Prosperity*.

3. Radelet, *Challenging Foreign Aid*. The twenty-two countries that have permanently graduated from IDA since 1960 are Botswana, Chile, China, Colombia, Costa Rica, Dominican Republic, Ecuador, Equatorial Guinea, El Salvador, Jordan, South Korea, Mauritius, Macedonia, Morocco, Papua New Guinea, Paraguay, St Kitts and Nevis, Swaziland, Syria, Thailand, Tunisia and Turkey.

4. Details of the Millennium Challenge Account can be found at http://www.mca.gov/about/index.php.

5. Sen, *Development as Freedom*.

6. Ferguson, *The Cash Nexus*, p. 349, refers to a study that compared the 'quality of citizens' lives' in over a hundred mainly developing countries and concluded that democratic states meet the basic needs of their citizens 'as much as 70 percent more' than non-democratic states.

7. The International Food Aid Conference VII, *Strengthening the Food Aid Chain*, was held on 3 May 2005 in Kansas City, Missouri.

8. Details of the Millennium Development Goals can be found at http://www.un.org/millenniumgoals/bkgd.shtml.

9. From *Foreign Exchange*, with Fareed Zakaria, on the US Public Broadcasting Service (PBS), 2 August 2007. Paul Collier, author of *The Bottom Billion*, cited a conversation in which this remark was made by the Chief Economist of the United Kingdom's Department of Trade and Industry, when Collier asked why the British charity continued with an aid campaign that was predicated on fundamentally poor economic analysis.

10. Easterly, 'Can Foreign Aid Buy Growth?'

4. The Silent Killer of Growth

1. *Economist*, 'Corruption in Kenya'.

2. See discussion at http://66.102.9.104/search?q=cache:guiKeYH5SgJ:www.transparency.org/content/download/4425/26684/file/08Legal hurdles.pdf+transparency+international+Mobutu+US%245+billion&hl=en&ct=clnk&cd=3&gl=uk.

3. Details on the EITI at http://eitransparency.org/.

4. Kurtzman, 'The Global Costs of Opacity'.

5. The comments were made by Senator Richard Lugar at the May 2004 United States Senate Committee on Foreign Relations hearing. Senator Lugar was chairing the first public hearing on corruption at the multilateral development banks.

6. Based on World Bank Uganda Public Expenditure Tracking Studies conducted between 1991 and 1995.

7. The disappearance of Mr Peter Mulamba, who was expected to be a key witness in two corruption trials around the grain debacle, was reported on the BBC News, 8 September 2004.

8. See the report by the UK's Africa All Party Parliamentary Group, 'The Other Side of the Coin: The UK and Corruption in Africa', March 2006, p. 14.

9. Collier, 'Natural Resources, Development and Conflict'.

10. Details of the peerage awarded to Lord Bauer can be found at http://www.parliament.uk/documents/upload/HLLPeerageCreation.pdf.

The Republic of Dongo

1. *Glasnost* refers to the policy of maximal publicity, openness and transparency in the activities of all government institutions in the Soviet Union, together with freedom of information. *Perestroika* referred to economic restructuring and economic reforms meant to overhaul the Russian economy.

5. A Radical Rethink of the Aid-Dependency Model

1. From PIPA, 'Americans on Foreign Aid and World Hunger: A Study of U.S. Attitudes', 2 February 2001, at http://65.109.167.118/pipa/pdf/feb01/ForeignAidFeb01rpt.pdf.
2. Statement of Peter Orszag, Director: 'Estimated Costs of U.S. Operations in Iraq and Afghanistan and of Other Activities Related to the War on Terrorism before the Committee on the Budget U.S. House of Representatives', 24 October 2007.

6. A Capital Solution

1. There exists also the BRVM, which is the regional stock exchange serving Benin, Burkina Faso, Guinea-Bissau, Ivory Coast, Mali, Niger, Senegal and Togo.
2. Details of the GEMLOC Program can be found at http://psdblog.worldbank.org/psdblog/2008/02/gemloc-program.html.
3. Details of the Pan African Infrastructure Development Fund (PAIDF) can be found at http://www.harith.co.za/.

7. The Chinese are Our Friends

1. Economists will realize that this point sweeps over wage arbitrage arguments. In practice, low wages do not necessarily imply low costs. What matters are not just wages, but wages relative to productivity,

that is, unit labour costs. Of course many low-wage countries actually have high unit labour costs because productivity is so low. However, one would expect that more rapid technological improvements across Africa would also lead to productivity improvements across the continent.

2. The World Bank's Doing Business Project provides objective measures of business regulations and their enforcement across 178 economies and selected cities at the subnational and regional level. See http://www.doingbusiness.org/.

3. Foreword to Kofi Annan (former Secretary-General of the United Nations), 'UNCTAD Foreign Direct Investment in Africa: Performance and Potential', New York, June 1999, at http://www.unctad.org/en/docs/poiteiitm1501.pdf.

4. For example, see *Africa Recovery*, 13 (1999), 2–3, p. 26 (part of a special feature on the ECA conference *Financing for Development*).

5. For more details on the Forum on China–Africa Cooperation, see http://www.focac.org/eng/.

6. China's January 2006 African Policy Investment Strategy. White Paper. China–Africa Cooperation Forum. China's Africa Policy. http://www.China.org.cn.

7. 'China in Africa', *Economist*.

8. Ibid.

9. In Ethiopia, Ivory Coast and Mali, 85, 72 and 81 per cent, respectively, see China's influence as growing as opposed to 73, 48 and 58 per cent, respectively, who see America's influence as growing.

10. Information on Zambia's Citizens Economic Empowerment Commission can be found at http://www.statehouse.gov.zm/index.php?option=comcontent&task=view&id=359&Itemid=45.

11. Information on the India–Africa Summit can be found at http://www.africa-union.org/root/au/Conferences/2008/april/India-Africa/India-Africa.html.

12. Information on the Fourth Tokyo International Conference on African Development can be found at http://www.mofa.go.jp/region/Africa/ticad/ticad4/index.html.

13. Information on Turkey's relationship with Africa can be found on http://www.tuskonafrica.com/en/cnt/stdcnt.php?anahtar=strateji.

14. Economist Intelligence Unit/CPII, 'World Investment Prospects to 2010'.

8. Let's Trade

1. Speech made by the World Bank's Chief Economist at the Centre for Economic Studies, Munich, Germany, November 2002.

2. Information on the African Growth and Opportunity Act can be found at http://www.agoa.gov/.

3. The countries eligible for AGOA are Benin, Botswana, Burkina Faso, Cameroon, Cape Verde, Chad, Ethiopia, Ghana, Kenya, Lesotho, Madagascar, Malawi, Mali, Mauritius, Mozambique, Namibia, Niger, Nigeria, Rwanda, Senegal, Sierra Leone, Swaziland, Tanzania, Uganda and Zambia.

4. Information on Everything But Arms can be found at http://ec.europa.eu/ trade/issues/global/gsp/eba/indexen.htm.

5. Paul Collier discussed the inequity between Europe's trade policy towards Somalia versus Kenya on *Foreign Exchange* with Fareed Zakaria, on the US Public Broadcasting Service (PBS) in August 2007.

6. Information on the India–Africa Summit can be found at http://www.africa-union.org/root/au/Conferences/2008/april/India–Africa/India–Africa.html.

7. This statistic comes from Learning Africa at http://www.learning africa.org.uk/generalfacts.htm.

9. Banking on the Unbankable

1. The Nobel Peace Prize 2006 was awarded to Muhammad Yunus and Grameen Bank 'for their efforts to create economic and social development from below'. See http://nobelprize.org/nobelprizes/peace/laureates/2006/.

2. More information on Grameen Bank can be found at http://www.grameen-info.org/.

3. More information on Kiva can be found at http://www.kiva.org/.

4. Vijay Mahajan, Managing Director of BASICS, estimated that 90 million farm holdings, 30 million non-agricultural enterprises and 50 million landless households in India collectively need approximately US$30 billion credit annually: http://www.uncdf.org/english/micro finance/pubs/newsletter/pages/200506/newsindia.php#fnote.

5. Ketkar and Ratha, Development Finance via Diaspora Bonds Track Record and Potential, 1 August 2007.

6. Adams and Page, 'Do International Migration and Remittances Reduce Poverty in Developing Countries?'

7. BBC News, 'Nigerian Boys Praised for Honesty', reported April 2005.

8. Giridharadas, 'India hopes to wean citizens from gold'.

10. Making Development Happen

1. In Landes, *The Wealth and Poverty of Nations*.

2. Perry, *Time* interview with Rwanda's President Kagame, September 2007.

3. Comments by President Abdoulaye Wade can be found at http://www.heritage.org/Press/Commentary/ed081602b.cfm and http://www.google.co.uk/search?hl=en&q=President+Wade+on+aid+free+markets&meta=.

4. From *Foreign Exchange* with Fareed Zakaria, on the US Public Broadcasting Service (PBS) in August 2007. Discussion with Paul Collier, author of *The Bottom Billion*.

5. Christopher Grimes, 'Can New York Defeat Poverty?' in *FT Weekend*, 24/25 May 2008. The idea of paying cash to the poor in exchange for better behaviour has been championed by the World Bank, which says conditional cash transfer programmes now exist in more than twenty countries. The World Bank and others recently launched a programme in Tanzania that pays fifteen- to thirty-year-olds almost US$50 a year to stay HIV-negative.

Bibliography

Adams, Richard H. and J. Page, 'Do International Migration and Remittances Reduce Poverty in Developing Countries?', *World Development*, 33 (2005), 10, pp. 1645–69

africaonline, 'Africa: Finance ministers state Africa's demands', 14 November 2001, at http://www.africaonline.com

Agency for International Development, Statistics and Reports Division, Marshall Plan Expenditure, 1975

Alden, E., 'Too little too late for US garment industry', *Financial Times*, 20 July 2004

Alesina, Alberto and David Dollar, 'Who Gives Foreign Aid to Whom and Why?', *Journal of Economic Growth*, 5 (2000), 1, pp. 33–63

Alesina, Alberto and Beatrice Weder, 'Do Corrupt Governments Receive Less Foreign Aid?', *American Economic Review*, 92 (2002), 4, pp. 1126–37

Allen, Tim and Diana Weinhold, 'Dropping the Debt for the New Millennium: Is It Such a Good Idea?', *Journal of International Development*, August 2000, pp. 857–76

Al-Marhubi, Fahim A., 'Corruption and Inflation', *Economic Letters*, 66 (2000), 2, pp. 199–202

Anderson, K., Copenhagen Consensus Challenge Paper, 'Subsidies and Trade Barriers', Centre for International Economic Studies, 2004, at www.copenhagenconsensus.com/ . . . /Filer/CC/Papers/Subsidies andTradeBarriers140504

Arslanalp, Serkan and Peter Blair Henry, 'Helping the Poor Help Themselves: Debt Relief or Aid?', NBER Working Paper No. 10230, January 2004

—, 'Debt relief: What do markets think?', NBER Working Paper No. 9369, 2002

—, 'Is Debt Relief Efficient?', *Journal of Finance*, 60 (2005), 2, pp. 1017–51

—, 'Policy Watch: Debt Relief', *Journal of Economic Perspectives*, 20 (2006), 1, pp. 207–20

Astier, Henri, 'Can aid do more harm than good?', updated 1 February 2006 at BBC News

Azam, Jean-Paul and Flore Gubert, 'Migrant Remittances and Economic Development in Africa: A Review of Evidence', *Journal of African Economies*, 15 (2006), 2, pp. 426–62

Baffes, John, *Cotton: Market Setting, Trade Policies, and Issues*, Washington DC: The World Bank, Development Prospects Group, 2004

Balls, Andrew, 'Aid will not lift growth in Africa, warns IMF', *Financial Times*, 30 June 2005

Balls, A., A. Beattie and C. Giles, 'Trade, aid and debt relief: Can this year's ambitious anti-poverty promises be kept?', *Financial Times*, 6 January 2005

Banerjee, Abhijit V., 'Making Aid Work: How to Fight Global Poverty – Effectively', *Boston Review*, July/August 2006

Barro, Robert J., 'Democracy and Growth', *Journal of Economic Growth*, 1 (1996), 1, pp. 1–27

Bartlett, Bruce, 'Peter Bauer, R.I.P.', *National Review Online*, 8 May 2002

Basu, Anupam, Rodolphe Blavy and Murat Yulek, 'Microfinance in Africa: Experience and Lessons from Selected African Countries', IMF Working Paper WP/04/174, September 2004

Bauer, Peter Thomas, *The Rubber Industry: A Study in Competition and Monopoly*, London: Longmans, Green & Co., 1948

—, *West African Trade: A Study of Competition, Oligopoly and Monopoly in a Changing Economy*, Cambridge: CUP, 1954

—, *Economic Analysis and Policy in Under-Developed Countries*, Cambridge: CUP, 1954

Baxter, Joan, 'Cotton subsidies squeeze Mali', 19 May 2003 at http://news.bbc.co.uk/1/hi/world/africa/3027079.stm

BBC News, 'Arms exports law to be changed', 6 December 2000, at http://news.bbc.co.uk/1/hi/ukpolitics/1057658.stm

—, 'African business gears up for trade meet', 29 October 2001, at http://news.bbc.co.uk/1/hi/business/1625919.stm

—, 'US grants African nations special tariffs', 3 January 2002

—, 'Zambia's ex-leader on theft charge', 24 February 2004

—, 'Europe unveils farm reform plans', 22 January 2003, http://news.bbc.co.uk/1/hi/world/europe/2685065.stm

Beattie, Alan, 'Sugar price cuts threaten Mozambique's sweet dreams', *Financial Times*, 10 March 2005

—, 'The truth behind the top five trade myths and why it matters', *Financial Times*, 1 July 2006

—, 'The Great Unknown', *Financial Times*, 8 July 2006

Beattie, A. and F. Williams, 'Who's for the WTO? Trade is troubled by divisions within the Developing World', *Financial Times*, 5 April 2005

Becker, Elizabeth, 'Wealthiest nations to increase aid to poorest', *The New York Times*, 23 February 2005

Beers, David T., Marie Cavanaugh and Takahira Ogawa, 'Sovereign Credit Ratings: A Primer', 3 April 2002, at http://www.securitization.net/pdf/SovereignCreditRatings3402.pdf

Blundell, John, et al., *A Tribute to Peter Bauer*, London: The Institute of Economic Affairs, 2002

Boone, Peter, 'Politics and the Effectiveness of Foreign Aid', *European Economic Review*, 40 (1996), 2, pp. 289–329

Booth, J., 'How to Keep Developing Countries in their Place: Cut Them Off from Capital', Ashmore Investment Management Ltd, 4 October 2001

—, 'Promoting Development', *Pension and Fund Management*, Winter 2002, at http://www.publicservice.co.uk/pdf/tlr/winter2002/p66.pdf

—, 'Emerging Market Local Currency Debt', AME Information, 23 September 2003

—, 'Emerging Market Debt: Asset Class Characteristics, Alpha Generation: The Case for Protection', Ashmore Investment Management Ltd presentation, 4 February 2005

Bordo, Michael D., 'Is There a Good Case for a New Bretton Woods International Monetary System?', *American Economic Review*, 85 (1995), 2, pp. 317–22, at http://links.jstor.org/sici?sici=00028282%28199505%2985%3A2%3C317%3AITAGCF%3E2.0.CO%3B2-A

BRAC, Ultra Poor Programme in Bangladesh, at http://www.brac.net

Braithwaite, John and Peter Drahos, 'Bretton Woods: Birth and Breakdown', Global Policy Forum, April 2001, at http://www.globalpolicy.org/socecon/bwi-wto/2001/braithwa.htm

Brenner, Reuven, *The Force of Finance: Triumph of the Capital Markets*, New York: Texere, 2002

Broadman, Harry G., *Africa's Silk Road: China and India's New Economic Frontier*, Washington, DC: The World Bank, 2007

Brookins, Carole, 'Anticorruption efforts of the MDBs', testimony before the Senate Foreign Relations Committee, 13 May 2004, JS-1550 at www.senate.gov/~foreign/testimony/2004/BrookinsTestimony040513.pdf

Bulow, Jeremy, 'First World Governments and Third World Debt', *Brookings Papers on Economic Activity* (2002), 1, pp. 229–55

Burkett, Paul, review of 'The Age of Diminished Expectations: U.S. Economic Policy in the 1990s', *Monthly Review*, October 1992

Burnett, John S., 'Relief workers in the line of fire', *International Herald Tribune*, 5 August 2004

Burnside, C. and D. Dollar, 'Aid, Policies, and Growth', *American Economic Review*, 90 (2000), 4

Casella, A. and B. Eichengreen, 'Can Foreign Aid Accelerate Stabilisation?', *Economic Journal*, 106 (1996), 436, pp. 605–19

Cassel, A., 'Why U.S. farm subsidies are bad for the world', *Philadelphia Inquirer*, 6 May 2002, at http://www.commondreams.org/views02/0506-09.htm

Christensen, Jakob, 'Domestic Debt Markets in Sub-Saharan Africa', IMF Working Paper WP/04/46, 2004, at http://www.imf.org/external/pubs/ft/wp/2004/wp0446.pdf

Claessens, S. and Kristin J. Forbes (eds.), *International Financial Contagion*, Boston: Kluwer, 2001

Clemens, Michael A., Steven Radelet and Rikhil Bhavnani, 'Counting Chickens When They Hatch: The Short-Term Effect of Aid on Growth', 2004, at http://ideas.repec.org/s/wpa/wuwpif.html

Clements, Benedict, Sanjeev Gupta, Alexander Pivovarsky and Erwin R. Tiongson, 'Foreign Aid: Grants versus Loans', *Finance and Development*, September 2004

CNN News, 'Mugabe's visit "distasteful"', 10 June 2002

Cobb Jr, Charles, 'Bush Administration Reduces Africa Aid Bid', Jubilee, Supporting Economic Justice Campaigns Worldwide, 25 October 2001

Collier, Paul, 'Natural Resources, Development and Conflict: Channels of Causation and Policy Interventions', The World Bank, April 2003

—, 'Africa: Geography and Growth', Centre for the Study of African Economies, Department of Economics, Oxford University, 2006, at http://www.kc.frb.org/publicat/sympos/2006/pdf/collier.paper.0901.pdf

—, *The Bottom Billion: Why the Poorest Countries are Failing and What Can be Done about It*, Oxford: OUP, 2007

Collier, Paul and Anke Hoeffler, 'Greed and Grievance in Civil War', Centre for the Study of African Economies, Department of Economics, Oxford University, March 2002, WPS 2000–18, at http://www.csae.ox.ac.uk/workingpapers/pdfs/2002–01text.pdf

—, 'On the Incidence of Civil War in Africa', *Journal of Conflict Resolution*, 46 (2002), 1, pp. 13–28

—, Copenhagen Consensus Challenge Paper, 'The Challenge of Reducing the Global Incidence of Civil War', Centre for International Economic Studies, 2004

Commission for Africa, 'Our Common Interest: Report for the Commission for Africa', 2005, at http://www.commissionforafrica.org/english/home/newsstories.html

Commission on Capital Flows to Africa, 'A Ten Year Strategy to Increase Aid Flow to Africa', June 2003, at http://www.iie.com/publications/papers/africa-report.pdf

Crocker, David A., 'Comments on Paul Collier, "Making Aid Smart," Institutional Reform in the Informal Sector', University of Maryland, Forum Series on the Role of Institutions in Promoting Growth/Market Augmenting Government, February 2002

Cross, John C., 'Development NGOs, the State and Neo-Liberalism: Competition, Partnership or Co-Conspiracy', The American University in Cairo, July 1997, at www.openair.org/cross/NGOS.htm

Cull, Robert, Asli Demirgüç-Kunt and Jonathan Murdoch, 'Microfinance Meets the Market', The World Bank Policy Research Working Paper WPS4630, May 2008

Dammasch, Sabine, 'The System of Bretton Woods: A Lesson from History', at http://www.ww.uni-magdeburg.de/fwwdeka/student/arbeiten/006.pdf

de Jonquières, Guy, ' "Few gains" from US move on Africa imports', *Financial Times*, 13 April 2004

—, 'Oxfam says EU sugar trade is hurting the poor', *Financial Times*, 14 April 2004

de Soto, Hernando, *The Mystery of Capital: Why Capitalism Triumphs in the West and Fails Everywhere Else*, New York: Basic Books, 2000

Delgado, Christopher L., Jane Hopkins and Valerie A. Kelly, 'Agricultural Growth Linkages in Sub-Saharan Africa', International Food Policy Research Institute, Research Report 107, 1998

Devarajan, Shanta and Vinaya Swaroop, 'The Implications of Foreign Aid Fungibility for Development Assistance', The World Bank Development Research Group Working Paper WPS2022, October 1998

Devarajan, S., A. S. Rajkumar and V. Swaroop, 'What Does Aid to Africa Finance?', The World Bank Development Research Group Working Paper WPS2092, August 1999

Diamond, Jared, *Guns, Germs and Steel: A Short History of Everybody for the Last 13,000 Years*, New York: Vintage, 1998

Diamond, Larry, 'Promoting Real Reform in Africa', in *Democratic Reform in Africa: The Quality of Progress*, ed. E. Gyimah-Boadi, Boulder, Colo.: Lynne Reinner, 2004, pp. 263–92

Diamond, L. and M. Plattner, *Democratization in Africa*, Baltimore: Johns Hopkins University Press, 1998

Dixon, Hugh, D. Griffiths and L. Lawson, 'Exploring Tradable and Non-Tradable Inflation in Consumer Prices', at www.stats.govt.nz/ . . . /7CE7312D-1230–447F-9360–4CD1BE08925E/0/Exploring TradableNonTradableInflationinCP.pdf

Djankov, Simeon, Caralee McLiesh and Rita Ramalho, 'Regulation and Growth', *Economic Letters*, 92, 3, pp. 395–401

Dollar, David, 'Outward-Oriented Developing Economies Really Do Grow More Rapidly: Evidence from 95 LDCs, 1976–1985', *Economic Development and Cultural Change*, 40 (1992), 3, pp. 523–44

Dollar, D. and A. Kraay, 'Trade, Growth, and Poverty', *International Monetary Fund*, 38 (2001), 3, at http://www.imf.org/external/pubs/ft/fandd/2001/09/dollar.htm

—, 'Trade, Growth, and Poverty', The World Bank Policy Research

Working Paper WPS2615, August 2002, at http://www.worldbank.org/research/growth/pdfiles/Trade5.pdf

Dornbusch, R., Yung Chul Park and Stijn Claessens, 'Contagion: How it spreads and how it can be stopped', The World Bank, May 2000, at http://www1.worldbank.org/economicpolicy/managing%20volatility/contagion/documents/Claessens-Dornbusch-Park.pdf

Doucouliagos, H. and Martin Paldam, 'Aid Effectiveness on Growth: A Meta Study', September 2006, at http://www.econ.au.dk/viphtm/mpaldam/Papers/MetaG.pdf

Easterly, William, 'Can Foreign Aid Buy Growth?', *Journal of Economic Perspectives*, 17 (2003), 3, pp. 23–48

Easterly, William and Ross Levine, 'Africa's Growth Tragedy: Policies and Ethnic Divisions', *Quarterly Journal of Economics*, 112 (1997), 4

Easterly, William, Ross Levine and David Roodman, 'New Data, New Doubts: A Comment on Burnside and Dollar's "Aid, Policies, and Growth (2000)"', 2003, at http://www.nyu.edu/fas/institute/dri/DRIWP/DRIWP04.pdf

Economides, G., S. Kalyvitis, and A. Philippopoulos, 'Does Foreign Aid Distort Incentives and Hurt Growth? Theory and Evidence from 75 Aid-Recipient Countries', *Public Choice*, 134 (2008), 3–4, pp. 463–88

Economist, 'Aid For Africa', 22 May 2002

—, 'Britain's Aid Policy', 31 October 2002

—, 'Dealing with Default', 8 May 2003

—, 'Argentina: IMF Default', Global Agenda, 10 September 2003

—, 'Poverty's Chains', 9 October 2003

—, 'An Emerging Crisis', Global Agenda, 3 February 2004

—, 'Free Trade's Best Friend', 20 January 2005

—, 'Recasting the Case for Aid', 20 January 2005

—, 'Corruption in Kenya: Feet of Clay', 10 February 2005

—, 'The Mystery of Capital Deepens', 24 August 2006

—, 'China in Africa', 26 October 2006

Economist Intelligence Unit and The Columbia Program on International Investment (CPII), 'World Investment Prospects to 2010: Boom or Backlash', 6 September 2006

Edwards, Sebastian, 'Trade Orientation, Distortions and Growth in

Developing Countries', *Journal of Development Economics*, Elsevier, 39 (1992), 1, pp. 31–57

EMTA, the Brady Plan, at http://emta.org/emarkets/brady.html

England, A., 'Trouble looms for Kenya as trade deal starts to unravel', *Financial Times*, 14 January 2005

England, Roger, 'Development goals perpetuate a failing system', *Financial Times*, 27 January 2005

European Union, 'Everything But Arms', at http://stats.oecd.org/glossary/detail.asp?ID=6763

Euroweek, 'Poland and Hungary Wave Farewell to Emerging Tags', no. 788, 31 January 2003

Ferguson, Niall, *Empire: How Britain Made the Modern World*, London: Penguin Books, 2004

—, *The Cash Nexus: Money and Power in the Modern World, 1700–2000*, New York: Basic Books, 2002

Financial Times, 'Prescriptions for a Continent's pain', 25 November 2004

—, 'Tanzania first to benefit from UK write-off', 14 January 2005

Fisman, Raymond and Jakob Svensson, 'Are Corruption and Taxation Really Harmful to Growth? Firm-Level Evidence', The World Bank Policy Research Working Paper WPS2485, November 2000

Forbes, Kristin J., 'The Asian Flu and Russian Virus: Firm Level Evidence on How Crises are Transmitted Internationally', NBER Working Paper No. W7807, July 2000

Foster, Mick and Adrian Fozzard, 'Aid and Public Expenditure: A Guide', Centre for Aid and Public Expenditure, Overseas Development Institute, Working Paper 141, October 2000

Freund, C. and N. Spatafora, 'Remittances: Transaction Costs, Determinants, and Informal Flows', The World Bank Policy Research Working Paper WPS3704, 2005

Genesis, 'Evolving Opportunities and Constraints in Remittances: A View from SADC', presentation at the 2nd International Conference on Migrant Remittances, London, November 2006

Gimbel, John, *The Origins of the Marshall Plan*, Stanford: Stanford University Press, 1976

Giridharadas, Anand, 'India hopes to wean citizens from gold', *Inter-*

national Herald Tribune, 16 March 2005, at http://www.iht.com/
articles/2005/03/15/news/gold.php.

Giuliano, Paola and Marta Ruiz-Arranz, 'Remittances, Financial Development, and Growth', IMF Working Paper Number WP/05/234,
December 2005

Graf Lambsdorff, Johann, 'How Corruption Affects Persistent Capital
Flows,' *Economics of Governance* (2003), 4, pp. 229–43

—, 'How Corruption Affects Productivity,' *Kyklos* (2003), 56, pp. 457–74

Grossman, H. I., 'Foreign Aid and Insurrection', *Defense Economics* (1992)
3, pp. 275–88

—, 'Kleptocracy and Revolutions', *Oxford Economic Papers* (1999), 51,
pp. 267–83

Guardian, 'Muddying the world's conscience', 9 January 2004

Hackett, W. T. G., 'Bretton Woods', The Canadian Institute of International Affairs (BLPES pamphlet collection), 1945

Hadjimichael, M. T., D. Ghura, M. Mulheisen, R. Nord and E. M.
Ucer, 'Sub-Saharan Africa: Growth, Savings and Investment, 1986–
93', IMF Occasional Paper No. 118, 2005

Hartung, William D. and Frida Berrigan, 'U.S. Arms Transfers and
Security Assistance to Israel: An Arms Trade Resource Center Fact
Sheet', 6 May 2002, at http://www.worldpolicy.org/projects/arms/
reports/israel050602.html

Harvard University, Washington Consensus, at http://www.cid.harvard.
edu/cidtrade/issues/washington.html

Hjertholm, Peter and Howard White, 'Foreign Aid in Historical Perspective: Background and Trends', in Tarp (ed.), *Foreign Aid and Development*

Huntington, Samuel, *Political Order in Changing Societies*, New Haven:
Yale University Press, 1968

Ibisin, David and Jake Lloyd Smith, 'Tsunami disaster: UN "failing to
co-ordinate relief efforts"', *Financial Times*, 7 January 2005

IFAD Remittance Forum, 'Sending Money Home: Worldwide Remittance Flows to Developing Countries', at http://www.ifad.org/
events/remittances/maps/

ING Microfinance Support, 'A Billion to Gain? A Study on Global
Financial Institutions and Microfinance', February 2006

International Monetary Fund, 'The IMF at a Glance: A Fact Sheet', at http://www.imf.org/external/np/exr/facts/glance.htm

—, Development Committee, 73rd Meeting, Washington, DC, April 2006, statement by Richard Manning, Chairman OECD DAC, at http://siteresources.worldbank.org/DEVCOMMINT/ Documentation/20898324/DCS2006–0006-OECD-DAC.pdf

International Peace Research Institute, Oslo (PRIO): http://www.prio.no/

Islam, Sirajul, 'Migration, Remittances and MFIs', *Jamaica Gleaner News*, 29 November 2006

Jamaica Gleaner News, 'Remittances encourage dependency over productivity – Davies', 22 November 2006

Kanbur, Ravi, 'Aid, Conditionality and Debt in Africa', in Tarp (ed.), *Foreign Aid and Development*

—, 'The Economics of International Aid', in ibid.

Kaur, H., 'US farm subsidies a blow to poor countries', *Third World Network*, 14 June 2002, at http://www.twnside.org.sg/title/twr141f.htm

Ketkar, Suhas L. and Dilip Ratha, 'Development Finance Via Diaspora Bonds: Track Record and Potential', The World Bank Policy Research Working Paper No. 4311, 1 August 2007

Knack, Stephen, 'Aid Dependence and the Quality of Governance: Cross-Country Empirical Tests', *Southern Economic Journal*, October 2001

Konare, Alpha O. and Peter McPherson, 'A partnership for Africa's future', *Wall Street Journal*, 18 October 2004, p. A19

Krugman, Paul, 'Competitiveness – A Dangerous Obsession', *Foreign Affairs*, March/April 1994, at http://www.foreignaffairs.org/19940301 faessay5094/paul-krugman/competitiveness-a-dangerous-obsession.html

Kurtzman, Joel, 'The Global Costs of Opacity – Measuring Business and Investment Risk Worldwide', *MIT Sloan Management Review*, October 2004

Kuziemko, Ilyana and Eric Werker, 'How Much is a Seat on the Security Council Worth? Foreign Aid and Bribery at the United Nations', *Journal of Political Economy*, 114, 5

Landes, David, *The Wealth and Poverty of Nations: Why Some are So Rich and Some So Poor*, New York: W. W. Norton & Company, 1999

Lau, J., 'HK Retains "World's Freest Economy" Ranking', *Financial Times*, 5 January 2005

Lienert, Ian, 'Civil Service Reform in Africa: Mixed Results After 10 Years', *Finance and Development*, 35 (1998), 2

Lindert, Peter. H. and Peter J. Morton, 'How Sovereign Debt has Worked', in Jeffrey D. Sachs (ed.), *Developing Country Debt and Economic Performance*, Vol. 1: *The International Financial System*, Chicago: University of Chicago Press, 1989

Littlefield, E., J. Murdoch and S. Hashemi, 'Is Microfinance an Effective Strategy to Reach the Millennium Development Goals?', CGAP Focus Note 24, January 2003

Lugar, Senator Richard, Senate Foreign Relations Committee, 13 May 2004. Chairman Richard Lugar, Opening Statement for Hearing on Combating Multilateral Development Bank Corruption: U.S. Treasury Role and Internal Efforts

Maren, Michael, *The Road to Hell: The Ravaging Effects of Foreign Aid and International Charity*, New York: Free Press, 1997

Masud, Nadia and Boriana Yontcheva, 'Does Foreign Aid Reduce Poverty? Empirical Evidence from Nongovernmental and Bilateral Aid', IMF Working Paper WP/05/100, May 2005

Mauro, Paolo, 'Corruption and Growth,' *Quarterly Journal of Economics*, 110 (1995), 3, pp. 681–713

Mauro, Paolo, N. Sussman and Y. Yafeh, *Emerging Markets and Financial Globalization: Sovereign Bond Spreads in 1870–1913 and Today*, New York: OUP, 2006

Mekay, E., 'Opponents unite to decry US farm subsidies', *Third World Network*, no. 280, 1–15 May 2002, at http://www.twnside.org.sg/title/twe280e.htm

Menon, A., 'The bitter truth about European sugar', *Financial Times*, 25 February 2005

Meredith, Martin, *The State of Africa: A History of Fifty Years of Independence*, New York: Free Press, 2006

Microfinance Bulletin, Microfinance Information eXchange, no. 15, Autumn 2007

Mishkin, Frederic S., *The Next Great Globalization: How Disadvantaged Nations Can Harness Their Financial Systems to Get Rich*, New Jersey: Princeton University Press, 2006

Mitchell, Donald, 'Sugar Policies: Opportunity for Change', The World Bank Policy Research Working Paper WPS3222, February 2004

Mlachila, Montfort and Yongzheng Yang, 'The End of Textiles Quotas: A Case Study of the Impact on Bangladesh', IMF Working Paper WP/04/108, June 2004

Moss, Todd, 'A Marshall Plan is not what Africa needs', *International Herald Tribune*, 29 December 2004, reprinted by the Centre for Global Development

Murdoch, Jonathan, 'The Microfinance Promise', *Journal of Economic Literature*, xxxvii (December 1999), pp. 1569–1614

Murphy, K., A. Schleifer and R. Vishny, 'Why is Rent-Seeking So Costly for Growth?', *The American Economic Review*, 83, 2, Papers and Proceedings of the 105th Annual Meeting of the American Economic Association (May 1993), pp. 409–14

Mwenda, A. M., 'Africa: Foreign Aid Sabotages Reform', *International Herald Tribune*, 8 March 2005

Naím, Moisés, 'Help Not Wanted', *The New York Times*, 15 February 2007

Nellis, John, 'Privatisation in Africa: What Has happened? What is to be Done?', Fondazione Eni Enrico Mattei, October 2005

Neumayer, E., 'The Determinants of Aid Allocation by Regional Multilateral Development Banks and United Nations Agencies', *International Studies Quarterly*, 47 (2003), pp. 101–22

North, Douglass, *The Economic Growth of the United States, 1790–1860*, Eaglewood Cliffs, NJ: Prentice-Hall, 1961

—, *Institutions, Institutional Change and Economic Performance*, Cambridge: CUP, 1990

Olson, Mancur, *Power and Prosperity: Outgrowing Communist and Capitalist Dictatorships*, Oxford: OUP, 2000

Olson, Mancur (with Martin C. McGuire), 'The Economics of Autocracy and Majority Rule: The Invisible Hand and the Use of Force', *Journal of Economic Literature*, March 1996

O'Neill, J., A. Bevan, T. Yamakawa and T. Miura, 'Refuting the JGB Downgrade: JGB's Deserve Aaa', Goldman Sachs Global Economics Paper No. 76, June 2006

Organisation for Economic Co-operation and Development, 'Untying Aid to the Least Developed Countries', Policy Brief, *OECD Observer*, 2001, at http://www.oecd.org/dataoecd/16/24/2002959.pdf

—, 'Aid flows top USD 100 billion in 2005', 4 April 2006, at http://www.oecd.org/document/40/0,2340,en2649201185364183441111, 00.html

—, 'Is It ODA?', Development Assistance Committee (DAC) Factsheet, May 2007, at http://www.oecd.org/dataoecd/21/21/34086975.pdf

Paloni, A. and Maurizio Zanardi (eds.), *Regional Aid Flows: The IMF, WB and Policy Reform*, London: Routledge, 2006

Parker, J., I. Singh and K. Hattel, 'The Role of Microfinance in the Fight against HIV/AIDS', UNAIDS United Nations Joint Programme on HIV/AIDS, 15 September 2000

Patricof, A., 'Trade not aid will meet Africa's challenges', *Financial Times*, 3 March 2005

Pearce, Kimber C., 'Rostow, Kennedy and the Rhetoric of Foreign Aid', East Lansing: Michigan State University Press, 2001

Perry, Alex, interview with Rwanda's President Kagame, *Time*, September 2007, at http://www.time.com/time/magazine/article/0,9171, 1666064,00.html

Pew Global Attitudes Project, report on 'Global Unease with Major World Powers', 27 June 2007

Polity IV Project, 'Political Regime Characteristics and Transitions, 1800–2006', at http://www.systemicpeace.org/polity/polity4.htm

Przeworski Adam, José Antonio Cheibub, Fernando Papaterra Limongi Neto and Michael M. Alvarez, 'What Makes Democracies Endure?', *Journal of Democracy*, 7 (1996), 1, pp. 39–55

Radelet, Steven, *Challenging Foreign Aid: A Policymaker's Guide to the Millennium Challenge Account*, Washington, DC: Center for Global Development, 2003

Rajan, Raghuram, 'Foreign Capital and Economic Growth', paper presented at a conference organized by the Federal Reserve Bank of Kansas City, Jackson Hole, Wyoming, 25 August 2006 (based on a paper written by Eswar Prasad, Raghuram Rajan and Arvind Subramanian)

Rajan, Raghuram G. and Arvind Subramanian, 'What Undermines Aid's Impact on Growth?', IMF Working Paper WP/05/126, 2005

—, 'Aid and Growth: What Does the Cross-Country Evidence Really Show?', IMF Working Paper WP/05/127, 2005

Ratha, Dilip, 'Remittances: A Lifeline for Development', *Finance and Development*, 42 (2005), 4

Ratha, D., S. Mohapatra and S. Plaza, 'Beyond Aid: New Sources and Innovative Mechanisms for Financing Development in Sub-Saharan Africa', The World Bank Development Prospects Group Working Paper WPS4609, April 2008

Reichel, R., 'Development Aid, Savings and Growth in the 1980s: A Cross-section Analysis', *Savings and Development*, 19 (1995), 3, pp. 279–96

Rodrik, Dani, *In Search of Prosperity*, Princeton, NJ: Princeton University Press, 2003

Rose-Ackerman, Susan, Copenhagen Consensus Challenge Paper, 'The Challenge of Poor Governance and Corruption', Centre for International Economic Studies, 2004

Ruhashyankiko, Jean François, 'Why Do Some Countries Manage to Extract Growth from Foreign Aid?', IMF Working Paper WP/05/53, March 2005

Sachs, Jeffrey, *The End of Poverty: Economic Possibilities for Our Time*, London: Penguin, 2005

Sachs, J. and A. Warner, 'Economic Reform and the Process of Global Integration', *Brookings Papers on Economic Activity* (1995), 1, pp. 1–118

Sachs, J. D. and J. W. McArthur, 'Millennium Project: A Plan for Meeting the Millennium Development Goals (MDG)', *The Lancet* (2005), 365, pp. 347–53, 12 January 2005, at http://www.earth.columbia.edu/news/2005/images/lancet012205.pdf

Sachs, J. D., J. W. Mcarthur, G. Schmidt-Traub, M. Kruk, Faye M. Bahadur and G. McCord, 'Ending Africa's Poverty Trap', *Brookings Papers on Economic Activity* (2004), 2, pp. 117–216, and at http://www.unmillenniumproject.org/documents/BPEAEndingAfricasPovertyTrapFINAL.pdf

Sanger, David. E., 'Bush plan ties foreign aid to free market and civic rule', *The New York Times*, 26 November 2002

Schreiner, Mark, 'A cost effectiveness analysis of the Grameen Bank', Overseas Development Institute, Center for Social Development, Washington University in St Louis, 2003

scienceinafrica, Integrated Regional Information Networks, 2002, 'Developing countries call for scrapping of farm subsidies', 27 August 2002, at http://www.scienceinafrica.co.za/2002/august/farm.htm

Sen, Amartya, *Development as Freedom*, New York: Anchor, 2000

Standard & Poor's, 'Sovereign Ratings in Africa', April 2007

Stiglitz, Joseph E. and Andrew Charlton, 'A Development Round of Trade Negotiations?', 2004, at http://www2.gsb.columbia.edu/faculty/jstiglitz/download/2004CharltonStiglitz.pdf

—, 'Aid for Trade: A Report for the Commonwealth Secretariat', March 2006

Stockholm International Peace Research Institute: http://www.sipri.org/

Strobbe, Francesco, 'The Role of Microfinance in Addressing the HIV/AIDS Pandemic in Zambia: The Rainbow Model Provides a Future for AIDS Orphans', European Central Bank, April 2005

Sturzenegger F. and J. Zettelmeyer, 'Sovereign Defaults and Debt Restructurings', in *Debt Defaults and Lessons from a Decade of Crises*, Cambridge, Mass.: MIT Press, 2006

Sutherland, P., 'The real trade barriers that hinder poor countries', *International Herald Tribune*, 29 January 2005

Svensson, J., 'When is Foreign Aid Policy Credible? Aid Dependence and Conditionality', *Journal of Development Economics* (2000), 61, pp. 61–84

—, 'Why Conditional Aid Does Not Work and What Can be Done about It', *Journal of Development Economics* (2003), 70, pp. 381–402

—, 'Foreign aid and rent-seeking', *Journal of International Economics*, 51 (2000), 2, pp. 437–61

Tarp, Finn (ed.), *Foreign Aid and Development: Lessons Learnt and Directions for the Future*, New York: Routledge, 2000

Tavares, José, 'Does Foreign Aid Corrupt?', *Economics Letters*, 2003

Tertius, Zongo, 'Cotton, Sugar, and Groundnuts: A Political Economy of Credibility', paper presented at the Annual Bank Conference on Development Economics, Europe, Paris, 15–17 May 2003

Thorbecke, Erin, 'The Evolution of the Development Doctrine and the

Role of Foreign Aid, 1950–2000', in Tarp (ed.), *Foreign Aid and Development*

Toxopeus, H. and R. Lensink, 'Remittances and Financial Inclusion in Development', United Nations University Research Paper No. 2007/49, August 2007, UNU-WIDER

Transparency International, Annual Report (various issues), at http://www.transparency.org/publications/publications/annualreports/annualreport2007

United Kingdom Department for International Development (DFID), 'BME Remittance Survey – Research Report Prepared by ICM', 27 July 2006

United Nations, Charter of Economic Rights and Duties of States, GA Res. 3281(xxix), UN GAOR, 29th Sess., Supp. No. 31 (1974) 50

—, 'Microfinance in Africa: Combining the Best Practices of Traditional and Modern Microfinance Approaches towards Poverty Eradication', at http://www.un.org/esa/africa/microfinanceinafrica.pdf

—, report by the Secretariat of the United Nations Conference on Trade and Development, UN, Geneva, 2002, at http://www.unctad.org/en/docs/tdr2002en.pdf

—, 'Resource Flows to Africa: An Update on Statistical Trends, between 2000 and 2003', at www.un.org/africa/osaa

—, 'Remittances to Africa overtake Foreign Direct Investment', at http://www.un.org/africa/osaa/press/Promoting%20International%20support%20for%20peace%20and%20development%20%85.pdf

US Government, Marshall Plan Congressional Record, 30 June 1947, at http://usinfo.state.gov/usa/infousa/facts/democrac/57.htm

—, African Growth and Opportunities Act 2000, at http://www.agoa.gov/

Vásquez, Ian, Testimony before the International Financial Institution Advisory Commission, United States Congress. 'The International Monetary Fund: Challenges and Contradictions', 28 September 1999

Vision of Humanity, 'Global Peace Index 2008'

Watkins, Kevin, 'Cultivating Poverty: The Impact of US Cotton Subsidies on Africa', Oxfam Briefing Paper, 2002

Wexler, Immanuel, *The Marshall Plan Revisited: The European Recovery Program in Economic Perspective*, London: Greenwood Press, 1983

White, Howard and A. Geske Dijkstra, *Beyond Conditionality: Programme Aid and Development*, London: Routledge (forthcoming)

Winters, Jeffrey A., 'Combating corruption in Multilateral Development Banks', Hearing before the Committee on Foreign Relations, United States Senate, One Hundred Eighth Congress, Second Session, 13 May 2004

Wood, Robert E., *From Marshall Plan to Debt Crisis: Foreign Aid and Development Choices in the World Economy*, Berkeley: University of California Press, 1986

World Bank, 'Why the Name IBRD?', at http://web.worldbank.org/WBSITE/EXTERNAL/EXTABOUTUS/EXTARCHIVES/0,,contentMDK:20113929~pagePK:36726~piPK:36092~theSitePK:29506,00.htm

—, anti-corruption website, at http://www.worldbank.org/anticorruption

—, World Development Indicators, various years

—, 'Migration, Remittances and Economic Development', presentation at the International Symposium on International Migration and Development, Turin, 28–30 June 2006

—, 'World Bank Structural and Sectoral Adjustment Operations: The Second OED Review', Operations Evaluation Department, Washington, DC, 1992

—, 'Adjustment Lending in Sub-Saharan Africa: An Update', Operations Evaluation Department, Washington, DC, 1997

World Economic Forum, 'Blended Value Investing: Capital Opportunities for Social and Environmental Impact', March 2006

Zambian Presidential Address to Parliament: President Levy Mwanawasa's address to the National Assembly, 11 July 2002

Acknowledgements

Writing this book has been a multi-year project. It has been a challenging, exhilarating, wonderful and exasperating journey. Along the way, I was fortunate enough to meet the right persons at the right time. In their own unique way, each person made an invaluable contribution, more than they realize.

Very early in the process, when the book idea was just germinating, I met Philip Gould. His candour and guidance and confidence in me played a central role in the production of this book. So too have a number of extremely valuable brainstorming sessions with Tim Sebastian.

After many years of searching, I then met Caroline Michel, who has been nothing less than an agent extraordinaire! Anyone who has had the privilege of working with her will know exactly what I mean.

Over the years, I have greatly benefited from the conscientious research support of a number of people. In alphabetical order, I owe a great debt of gratitude to Steve Donze, Selim Gulesci, Gokce Hagnesten, Fatima Khan, Peter Nthepe, and Michael Wang. They have, in their own individual ways, left an indelible mark on the project.

In the spring of 2008, at what was arguably the most treacherous part of my whole book-writing process, I met Tim Binding. Without Tim, this book might never have been completed. I thank him for his patience and encouragement when I needed it most.

I have incorporated a range of excellent comments from Geordie Young, Peter Henry, Willem Buiter, Niall Ferguson and Rory Macfarquhar. This is without attribution. All errors and omissions are my own.

An enormous amount of gratitude is also due to the meticulous publishing team at Penguin. My editor, Will Goodlad, Gina Luck in Sales, Mark Handsley for thorough copy-editing, Nicola Hill, Jessica Price, and Pen Volger, all of whom had an important hand in getting the book from my mind to publication. And of course the publishing team at Farrar, Straus, and Giroux: Jonathan Galassi, Eric Chinski and Eugenie Cha have been nothing short of fantastic.

I thank Iris Mwanza, my oldest and dearest friend, for her indulgence. She was always there as I suffered and revelled at different stages of the expedition.

Finally, to my parents, Steven and Orlean Moyo, for their unwavering belief in me (and our continent Africa) every step of the way, even when there have been many reasons not to believe.

Index